PREHISTORIC ART

PREHISTORIC ART

*Including some recent cave-culture discoveries
and subsequent developments up to Roman times*

Photographs and graphic arrangement by

W. and B. FORMAN

Text by

JOSEF POULÍK

Translated by

R. FINLAYSON SAMSOUR

SPRING BOOKS · LONDON

Nine years ago, when we began work on this book, our co-author, friendly adviser and teacher was Academician Dr Jaroslav Böhm, vice-president of the Czechoslovak Academy of Science and director of the State Archaeological Institute.

We are indebted to the above for countless days of work in collaboration both in the repositories of scientific institutes and in the field.

Our thanks, besides going out to all who helped us in our work, are therefore due above all to him.

W. and B. Forman

Designed and produced by Artia for
SPRING BOOKS · SPRING HOUSE · SPRING PLACE · LONDON N. W. 5.
(S/B 77a)
Printed in Czechoslovakia

CONTENTS

LIST OF ILLUSTRATIONS

Palaeolithic or Old Stone Age

1. Stylised female figure engraved on a mammoth's tusk.
2. Pregnant woman seated (Venus).
3. Pendant with large, single knob.
4. Statuette of a mammoth.
5. Reconstruction of model of a mammoth.
6. Female statuette.
7. Female statuette.
8. Stylised female figures.
9. Female torso.
10. Male statuette.
11. Head of a female figure.
12. Head of a female figure.
13. Statuette of a bear.
14. Lioness's head.
15. Horse's head and mane.
16. Rhinoceros's head.
17. Model of a bear's head.
18. Extended head of a reindeer.
19. Drawing of an antelope's head.
20. Drawing of a horse.

Neolithic or New Stone Age

21. Large globular vessel.
22. Globular vessel with four zoomorphic lugs.
23. Bowl-shaped vessel.
24. Gourd-shaped vessel.
25. Bottle.
26. Human figure incised on a pot.
27. Figurine—function and purpose unknown.
28. Globular vessel.
29. Globular vessels.
30. Pear-shaped vessel with three high handles.
31. Pear-shaped vessel.
32. Bucket-shaped vessel.
33. Moulded bull's head.
34. Vessel on a hollow pedestal.
35. Bowl on a low foot.
36. Tripartite vessel on a human foot.
37. Vessel with vertically perforated lug-handles.
38. Vessel with well-preserved painted decoration.
39. Hooked ladle.
40. Vase with zoomorphic lugs and human figures in pricked technique.
41. Square vessel with feet.
42. Amphora-shaped vessels.
43. Vessel with tall neck—decorated with three knobs on widest part.
44. Bowl with four decorative horns.
45. Cubical object with a round hollow in the middle.
46. Female figurines showing extreme stylisation and exaggeration of the lower parts.
47. Stylised female figure.
48. Torso of a stylised female figure.
49. Human figure with stylisation of hair-dress.
50. Human figure with stylised hair-dress.
51. Female statuette.
52. Detail of the statuette.
53. Expressive stylised female figure with holes in the eye-sockets.
54. Small model of a human head.
55. Small heads modelled in clay.
56. Animal figurine with flat back containing a round opening.
57. Animal figurine with flat back containing a round opening.
58. Zoomorphic vessel representing a boar (bear?).
59. Handle of a vessel in the form of an animal.
60. Broken-off lug of a lid.
61. Prehistoric model of a hut with a gabled roof.

Chalcolithic or Late Stone Age

62. Jug with tall neck and shallow, flattened body.
63. Vase.
64. Small jug with a broad handle.

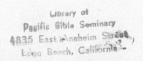

65. Cylindrical vessel with everted rim.
Vessel with four horns at widest part.
66. Gourd-shaped dish.
67. Dish on a foot.
68. Vessel with a strongly-marked bulge, decorated with plastic ribs.
69. Low jug decorated on the body with plastic ribs.
70. Jug with handle of the 'ansa lunata' type.
71. Vessel with finely smoothed surface.
72. Stylised animal head.
73. Upper part of amphora richly decorated.
74. Thin-walled vessel decorated with cord impressions.
75. Jug with broad handle and incised decoration.
76. Jug.

Early to Late Bronze Age

77. Cup decorated with fine slip.
78. Cups with widely everted rims and flattened bodies.
79. Vase with everted rim.
80. Two-handled vessel with perforated base —sieve— and waisted jug.
80a. Vessel with incised and white incrusted ornament.
81. Bone ring decorated with bands of wavy ornament in relief.
82. Two-handled vessel with vertical ribs on the body.
83. Jug with everted rims.
84. Small jug with everted rim, curved neck and well-preserved white incrustation.
85. Vase with one small perforated lug.
86. Jug with everted rim.
87. Biconical vessel with rough channeling on lower part.
88. Two-handled amphora with two perforated lugs and vertical ribs in relief.
89. Bottom of a vessel with rich relief, grooved and incised decoration.
90. Zoomorphic vessel.
91. Biconical vessel with lid.
92. Model of a booted human foot.
93. Cast sword hilt with relief and incised decoration.
94. Sword hilt, finely engraved.
95. Massive bronze bracelet with straight ends, the coils being reinforced with a moulded mid-rib.
96. Massive bronze bracelet.
97. Massive spiral ornament.
98. Massive personal ornament.

99. Splendid spiral brooch.
100. Tall conical helmet.
101. Rectangular plaque decorated with fine engraving.
102. Cup with ribbon handle.
103. Small vessel on human feet with high-set handles.
104. Knife with curved back and engraved design.

Hallstatt—Early Iron Age

105. Zoomorphic vessel ornament with pricked and grooved design.
106. Amphora with polished graphite surface.
107. Cup decorated on the outside with tin open-work.
108. Bracelet ending in a double pair of embossed (repoussé) spirals.
109. Front of a massive brooch.
110. Double vessel with single handle.
111. Double vessel joined at the body with a horizontal handle.
112. Fragment of a zoomorphic cult object from a hearth (?).
113. Zoomorphic vessel with slightly deformed body.
114. Low jug with grooved decoration.
115. Bracelet of bronze with tapering ends. Engraved design on outer side.
Massive lobed bracelet.
116. Bone object, function and purpose unknown, engraved with scene of a chariot drawn by a pair of horses.
117. Stylised figure of a horse.
118. Cast of a small bull figurine.
119. Rim of a plate decorated with stylised swans and sun symbols.
120. Stylised swan with two pendants below the beak.
121. Various vessels.
122. Pendant in the form of an animal.

La Tène Culture

123. Small metal plaque decorated with fine engraving and a grotesque human face.
124. Zoomorphic brooch with traces of enamel.
125. Sherds decorated with fine engraved and pricked design.
126. Amphora and two jugs.
127. Three bracelets and two richly ornamented brooches.

128. Piece of metal-work, with grotesque and caricatured human face.
129. Sculpture of a man's head.
130. Piece of metal-work, with exaggerated stylised animal figure.
131. Piece of metal-work with bird's head.
132. Deep pedestalled dish.
133. Bottle with polished surface.
134. Broad bottle with polished surface.
135. Large vase with incised decoration.
136. Statuette of a boar.
137. Stylised and elongated animal figure.
138. Small figure carrying unidentified tool.
139. Celtic coin found in Bohemia.
140. Small dog and boar designed as pendants.

Contact with the Roman Empire

141. Bronze flagon with female figurine (detail).
142. Bronze flagon with female figurine (general view).
143. Dish on a tall stem.
144. Tile with stamp of the XVth Legion.
145. Sherd with incised figure of a running animal.
146. Vessel with slightly inverted rims, decorated with typical arcade pattern.
147. Dish with raised moulded knobs and rough plaiting.
148. Bowl.
149. Brooches richly decorated with granulation.
150. Metal top on a glass goblet.
151. Glass dish.

Period of the 'Migration of Peoples'

152. Jar with broad flat rim.
153. Bowl with incised ornament.
154. Clasp with notched decoration.
155. Jug.
156. Fragment of ornament with plaited design.
157, 158, 159. Fragments of a pyxis decorated with figures.

160. Jewellery from the Migration Period.
161. Slender jug with massive handle.
162, 163. Helmet with gold and silver-plated parts, of copper (bronze?).

The Oldest Slavs

164. Vase of the Prague Type.
165, 166. Two-handled vessel and jug of fine loess and well-baked clay.
167, 168. Simple pottery built up by hand with incised ornament.
169. Barrel-shaped vessel with everted rim and incised design.
170. Shallow vessel of well-baked clay.
171, 172. Gilded bronze metal-work, with ornament showing zoomorphic stylisation.

Slavs from the IXth to the XIIth century

173. Slender vessel decorated with three parallel bands of engraved wavy lines.
174. Vessel with expressively profiled neck and incised wavy line.
175. Two-handled bottle.
176. Iron-work on an oval bucket and flat flask.
177. Iron-work on wooden bucket.
178. Bone pipe with engraved ornament.
179. Silver finger-ring and gold ear-rings, richly beaded.
180. Slav jewellery. Finger-ring and ornamental button.
181. Back of a gold pendant set with an antique cameo.
182. Finely engraved clasp.
183. Gold-plated silver chalice.
184. Buckle-plate and buckle-bow, richly decorated with silver embossed metal-work.
185. Badly damaged bone-urn (ossuary), with embossed deer and bird.
186. Zoomorphic vessel.
187. Silver Agnus Dei.
188. Bronze sculpture: The Crucified Man.
189. Bone comb, decorated with figures.

COLOUR PLATES

The geographical situation of Czechoslovakia in the heart of Europe has been a basic factor in the economic and social development of this territory from the earliest times. As in the case of neighbouring European regions, we mainly depend for a knowledge of the national history on literary sources which, however, document only the relatively short period of the two thousand years of the Christian era. Human history in the region goes back very much further, as is proved by numerous discoveries of domestic sites and burial places, in which tools, weapons and ornamental objects made of stone, bone, bronze and iron have been preserved. Such sites have been investigated in Czechoslovakia since the end of the eighteenth century. Investigations were first carried out more systematically and intensively, however, in the period 1918—1938, that is, up to the time of the Second World War. In the course of these investigations, the archaeologists acquired a large quantity of valuable material and information for the reconstruction not only of Czechoslovak but also of European prehistory from the Old Stone Age up to the period when the earliest Slavs founded their first settlements in these territories.

During the German occupation, the work of all our scientists, and so also of our archaeologists, was considerably restricted. Excavations of Slav and pre-Slav sites were not resumed till after the Liberation in 1945. The greatest advance in this field was achieved, however, after February 1948, when the Czechoslovak Government assigned to this branch of research such generous financial means as earlier generations of archaeologists would never have dreamed of. We were thus enabled to proceed with extensive investigations and research. These investigations, carried out with up-to-date technical equipment and with the co-operation of scientific workers from related fields of research, fully confirmed the historic value of the archaeological finds which are the individual and social product of man's labour in the various periods of prehistory.

Of the oldest known human industries represented by the so-called hand axes of the Abbevillian-Acheulian cycles, only doubtful traces have been found in Czechoslovakia, as in the rest of Central and Eastern Europe. The first coherent assemblages of humanly fashioned stone implements belong to the Mousterian culture (so called after a cave in the Dordogne). The race of men who used them as weapons against the cave bear has been called the Neanderthal stock — *Homo primigenius* — after a site near Düsseldorf in West Germany. Neanderthal Man was as yet far from fully developed. He had a low receding forehead, massive supraorbital ridges, a broad nose and no chin. Thus he did not yet speak an articulate language. These physical features of the Neanderthal Man, whose skeletal remains have been found in several places in both Eastern and Western Europe, in Asia and in Africa, prove that his efforts were devoted to defending his existence in his rude natural surroundings and in providing himself with the vegetable and animal food necessary for his sustenance.

Sites occupied by Neanderthal Man have also been found in the limestone caves of Czechoslovakia.

Among the best-known Czechoslovak sites, which are usually listed in general archaeological and anthropological literature, is the Šipka Cave near the town of Štramberk in eastern Moravia. In addition to stone tools of simple form, the finds include part of a child's jaw, of Neanderthal type. Finds of animal bones prove that these early cave-dwellers, who were already able to light fires and keep them going, were mainly engaged in the hunting of bears. Knowledge of the life of prehistoric peoples on the territories of Czechoslovakia—and this is true also of the nearer and more distant regions of Europe, Asia and Africa—as deduced from the sites so far investigated, is still very incomplete and uneven, and will for long continue to be the subject of scientific research by archaeologists, geologists and anthropologists.

So far it is not possible to trace the development of the physical features of the Neanderthal Man and his culture, evidence of which he left in the cave strata, along with piles of bear's bones. There can be no doubt, however, that the continual struggle he waged with his natural surroundings for survival led him to think of ways of improving his tools and weapons. Thus his brain activity was stimulated and work must have played a very significant role in developing the physical traits and mental faculties of prehistoric man. It is equally certain, however, that the advance of the Neanderthal Man to a higher human type must be measured in thousands of years. In Czechoslovakia, skeletons and graves of modern man's immediate fore-runners, belonging to the so-called Cro-Magnon race, are rather numerous in comparison with other European countries. In the neighbourhood of the town of Beroun, at the 'Zlatý kůň' (Golden Horse) Cave not far from Prague, in Brno, at Předmostí near Přerov, at Dolní Věstonice in southern Moravia, at Mladeč near Litovel and elsewhere, human skeletons have been found which differ conclusively from those of the cave-bear hunters, the Neanderthalers. They are more evolved, and it is indeed likely that these inhabitants of this land had already used an articulate speech and resembled modern men in all essentials.

Archaeological investigations have also discovered on Czechoslovak territory, in addition to the above-mentioned graves and human skeletons belonging to the *Homo sapiens* type, numerous domestic sites and camping-places. On the basis of geological observations, these belong to the last period of the Ice Age, roughly between 70,000 and 25,000 B. C. These sites are situated on hill-tops, and many of them were overlaid at the end of the Ice Age with immense layers of yellow loess. Traces of human habitation from this period have also been found in numerous limestone caves. The greatest number of sites of *Homo sapiens* is concentrated in the central part of the Czechoslovak territories—in Moravia. Besides a number of others, there are two very celebrated sites, one being Předmostí near Přerov, and the other Dolní Věstonice, in southern Moravia. The camping-place at Předmostí is situated at the confluence of the rivers Bečva and Morava, that is, on one of the important routes along which peoples of different racial and ethnical stock, and trade caravans, have passed since the earliest times from the north southwards to the Danube. These sites have been investigated since the end of last century, and it has been ascertained that life in them was concentrated especially in the region of limestone rocks covering about ten thousand square metres. Here an assemblage was found of up to 40,000 flint artifacts, and, in addition, numerous bone implements such as awls, daggers, spoons, fish-hooks etc., the material used being bones of the cave lion and the mammoth. Judging from the bones, the Předmostí hunters seem to have consumed about 600 mammoths. Besides stone and bone implements and weapons, objects were found testifying to a not inconsiderable mental activity on the part of their makers and providing numerous documents of their religious beliefs and aspirations to beauty and refinement. The statuette of a woman carved out of mammoth bone is well known, as are the figurine of a mammoth and the remarkable stylisation of a female figure carved on a mammoth's tusk.

A rather unusual find in this site of hunters of the Old Stone Age is a collective grave. In it were found the skeletons of 20 men, women and children, in contracted and extended positions. The grave was enclosed by limestone slabs, and the bodies had been covered with mammoth shoulder-blades. This grave of Pleistocene Man evoked great interest not only among scientists in Czechoslovakia, but among leading scientists throughout the world. A study of the remains proved that they belonged to the type of *Homo sapiens*. In anthropological literature, frequent mention is made also of the Předmostí Man, *Homo předmostensis*. For many decades the human skeletons from Předmostí, as well as the many notable finds from Brno and Mladeč in Moravia, were housed in the Moravian Museum in Brno. During the German occupation they were removed, for safety, along with other rare finds from the sites of the hunters of the Old Stone Age, to the cellars of Mikulov Castle in southern Moravia, near the Austrian frontier. When it was known that the Soviet Army was advancing on southern Moravia, the Nazis gave orders for the cellars to be soaked with paraffin and started a huge fire in which everything perished. Thus a criminal and barbarous act destroyed unique scientific material for the solution of fundamental problems relating to the life and culture of people of the Old Stone Age, not only of significance for Czechoslovakia but a common possession of humanity.

Along with the finds from Předmostí and other sites stored in the above-mentioned Castle at Mikulov were numerous stone implements and weapons from the extensive camping-place at Dolní Věstonice, which shared the same fate. This early site of human habitation is situated on the eastern slope of the Pavlov Heights, which rise from the South Moravian plain above the confluence of the rivers Svratka and Dyje. They are visible from a great distance, and have served, from the earliest times, as a natural landmark for travellers passing through the Moravian Gates and following the course of the river Morava south to the Danube, or for those travelling along the same route to the north. Archaeologists have ascertained that their slopes and the area in their vicinity were relatively densely populated throughout all periods of prehistory and formed a focal centre of development for autochthonous cultures. It is a fertile region providing favourable conditions for settlement. Thus the enterprising hunters of the Old Stone Age also reached this region and made it their camping place. Usually they are referred to as *mammoth-hunters*, for both at Předmostí and at Dolní Věstonice great quantities of mammoth bones are the proof that their source of food was mammoth hunting.

The site of the mammoth-hunters at Dolní Věstonice has long been known to science. It is situated deep below layers of yellow loess, which were deposited at the end of the last Ice Age, about 20,000 B. C., covering up all trace of the varied life which once flourished there. Scientific investigation of the site was carried out in the years 1924—1938, under the direction of the well-known archaeologist, Dr Karel Absolon, in the course of which large assemblages of flint and bone implements and weapons were found, as well as complete and fragmentary figures of animals such as the bear, lion, rhinoceros, horse, mammoth, fox etc. These are modelled in clay and baked. Proof of the artistic aspirations of the hunters on the Dolní Věstonice site is that notable find, the so-called Věstonice Venus. It is modelled in yellow brick-clay mixed with ash from burnt mammoth bones. A still greater surprise was the discovery of a human portrait carved from a mammoth's tusk. Bone objects were also found with rich incised geometrical patterns, necklaces of shells and perforated animal teeth.

After the Liberation of Czechoslovakia in the spring of 1945, more extensive archaeological investigations were initiated at Dolní Věstonice and have been carried on, especially since 1948, on a large scale.

These extensive excavations are generally planned to gain a deeper insight into the life and culture of the earliest inhabitants of Czechoslovak territory in the Old Stone Age. This orientation of the investigation has already produced remarkable and unexpected results. Of special interest is the discovery of the ground-plans of several dwellings covered with simple roofs. The plan is either round or oval and contains several hearths. In the neighbourhood of the hearths numerous stone and bone implements were found as well as animal figures of baked clay. Quite recently another figurine of a woman has come to light carved out of a mammoth's tusk. Not far from the dwellings a large midden was excavated containing mammoth bones. At the edge of one of them a grave was found with the skeleton of a woman interred in a contracted position, lying on her right side and covered with two mammoth shoulder-blades. Her skull showed traces of red colour. It is the skeleton of a woman of about 40, of the *Homo sapiens* type.

The investigations carried out within the last few years on the eastern slopes of the Pavlov Heights, beside the village of Dolní Věstonice, show that here the mammoth-hunters had a very extensive settlement covering some four square kilometres. Its thorough investigation will require the work of several generations of archaeologists. Indeed, a great deal of work awaits the scientific workers engaged in the study of the life, social organization and culture of Stone Age Man, for, especially in the central regions of Czechoslovakia—in Moravia and Silesia—there is a relatively large number of sites of mammoth-hunters similar to that at Dolní Věstonice. In this connection, we may mention the site at Petřkovice near Ostrava, situated on a hill above the river Odra. This site, too, lies beneath a deposit of yellow loess. Excavations revealed numerous stone implements and weapons and the unique statuette of a woman carved in haematite. In its general conception it is, in many respects, not unlike a present-day sculpture.

The finds made on the sites of the mammoth-hunters are evidence that these inhabitants of Czechoslovak territory had reached a fairly high level of development. The shapes of the implements and hunting tools are much more varied and functionally effective than those which the bear-hunters had been able to make. Thus the finds from the Czechoslovak camping-places and sites of the mammoth-hunters belong to the stage of the familiar Upper Aurignacian culture, known also as the Gravettian. These more advanced products are evidence of a further development of man's intellectual faculties. The next step was thus taken in which man not only produced implements for use, but began to pay some attention to their appearance by ornamenting them with geometric and animal motifs. They are, therefore, the record of man's oldest art and, as such, are closely connected with the life and conceptions of these primitive communities. Many of these artistic representations are inspired by the desire for success in the hunt. This is to be seen most clearly in several sculptures of animals bearing the magic signs for wounds. Magic played an important part in the lives of the hunters, as is strikingly documented on the walls of French and Spanish caves. In general conception, the artistic expression of the mammoth-hunters, as embodied in the finds from the Czechoslovak sites, shows eastern affinities.

The severe climatic conditions prevailing in the last Ice Age forced the hunters to live in communities. The basis of social organization at that time was the maternal family or *gens*, for, in it, woman had a very important status. While the men were engaged in hunting and in the making of implements and hunting gear, the women did all the work on the site. The function of the woman-mother in primitive society is attested by the above-mentioned finds of statuettes fashioned in various materials. It is interesting that the early artist represented certain parts of the body quite schematically. Thus the head is executed only quite roughly and the face is practically without expression, indeed, in some cases the head is altogether lacking. In the sculptures of female figures from the Czechoslovak sites, the whole upper part of the body is similarly without expression. On the other hand, the hips and those parts of the body closely connected with the idea of fertility are strikingly exaggerated. Occasionally the Old Stone Age artist attempted very daring stylisations of the female body, as witness the finds at the Dolní Věstonice site of the mammoth-hunters. Or, otherwise, in carving the figure of a woman in mammoth ivory, he would exaggerate those parts of the body in which new life is born. Only quite exceptionally did the sculptor belonging to the mammoth-hunting community produce the figure of a male, but such an attempt is documented by a rare find in a grave in Brno.

It will require long and patient study until it can be affirmed with any certainty how long the fires burned on the camping-places of the mammoth-hunters on Czechoslovak territory and elsewhere in Europe. Certain it is that it was a period of many thousands of years and that not even unfavourable climatic changes, causing the severest possible conditions of existence, were able to conquer man's will to survive. At that time, about 20,000 years ago, the climate of Central Europe was cold and dry. Tundra and taiga covered most of the land. Big game such as mammoth and rhinoceros were now succeeded by herds of reindeer. Man retreated from his settlements on open ground to the warmth of his hearth in limestone caves. The place of mammoth-hunters was taken by reindeer-hunters. Their cave dwellings are concentrated in the so-called Moravian Karst, not far from Brno. Among these sites an important place in the archaeological literature dealing with this period is occupied by the Pekárna Cave, near the village of Mokrá. The site was investigated in the years 1925 to 1930 by Prof. Dr Karel Absolon, of whom mention has already been made. In this cave, which derives its name from its similarity to a large oven or bake-house, a section has been cut and investigated, in the lowest layer of which are remains of a domestic site of mammoth-hunters of the Aurignacian culture. The next stratum shows that the cave was not inhabited for a long period, and only round about 20,000 B. C., at the end of the last Ice Age, did reindeer-hunters again set up their hearths here. Their stone and bone implements are part of the culture to which archaeology has given the name Magdalenian, after the site of La Madeleine in the Dordogne in France.

As in other sites of this period of Czechoslovak prehistory, in the Pekárna Cave, too, numerous flint implements have been found, some of which were inserted into bone hafts. Many implements and hunter's tools were found made of bone. They are more practical and suited to their purpose than those made by the mammoth-hunters, and thus represent another step forward in human progress. Among the notable finds are harpoons of reindeer antler. They are triple-barbed and served for the hunting of reindeer. An unique find in the Czechoslovak territory are so-called *bâtons* made of bone and perforated at one end. Numerous analogies exist among the finds from French sites. Evidence of the creative artistic urge among reindeer-hunting communities, is the celebrated find of a horse's rib on which a representation of a combat between three bison is delicately carved. Connected with this same desire for artistic expression, which here, too, has its roots to a great extent in hunting magic, are engravings on large flat pebbles. In the Pekárna Cave, as at the encampment of the mammoth-hunters near Dolní Věstonice, finds have been made of female figures carved in mammoth ivory.

While our knowledge of the life and culture of the first inhabitants of Czechoslovakia is still dim and uncertain, we are relatively better informed how the mammoth- and reindeer-hunters of the last Ice Age lived roughly between 70,000—15,000 years ago. The end of this epoch in the history of Czechoslovak territory, and of human history in general, still remains far from clear. Scientific research has shown that, somewhere around 15,000 B. C., considerable changes must have taken place in climatic conditions due to the melting of the icefields, which reached as far as the northern border ranges, and the consequent retreat northwards of the ice barrier. In the same way, the glaciers receded from the plains to higher elevations, and with them disappeared from these parts big game such as the mammoth, the reindeer and the woolly rhinoceros. The gradual retreat of the glaciers meant warmer and drier summers throughout Central Europe, and so also in this territory, and the region assumed quite a different aspect. Some time about 10,000 B. C., deciduous forests appeared in higher altitudes and alder groves flourished in the vicinity of water courses. In this altered natural environment, archaeologists have discovered more human settlements, now situated as a rule on moderately elevated, sandy ground in the neighbourhood of rivers and lakes. These sites belong to the Transitional Stone Age known as the Mesolithic Age, and a considerable number have been identified on Czechoslovak territory. Excavations carried out within the last few years, at Ražice in South Bohemia and elsewhere, provide evidence that the Mesolithic inhabitants dug their dwellings in the ground and covered them over with a gable roof. Hearths were found in the huts and stone anvils round which lay a large number of small stone artifacts. Here production was evidently concentrated.

Finds from the Mesolithic Age on Czechoslovak territory are attributed to the so-called Tardenoisian culture, named after the type site, Fère-en-Tardenois, in the north of France. The finds in this country show that Mesolithic Man engaged mainly in fishing and hunting game and fowl. His implements and hunting tools were also adapted to these activities. He was familiar with the bow and had domesticated the dog. The material culture of these communities is evidence that production and man's powers of thought had again made a notable advance. The finds so far made do not, however, allow of a deeper insight into the conceptions, beliefs and social structure of these communities of early hunter-fishers. The basis of society remained, in this period, too, the maternal family, which continued as the form of social organization throughout the next period of human history, the New Stone Age or the Neolithic Age.

On the uplands and slopes above streams and rivers, where at the end of the Ice Age there remained deposits of yellow loess, sites have been discovered on Czechoslovakian territory of which the material culture differs from that of the Mesolithic fishers and hunters. In addition to small flint implements, there are also larger objects for the making of which another kind of stone was used. In shape they resemble adzes, with one edge sharpened and with a perforated hole in which a wooden handle was inserted. In those early times they served both as an effective weapon and as a useful implement. From the finds in the strata of the above-mentioned sites on loess-uplands, it may be inferred that their inhabitants could make primitive sickles by inserting a sharp flint blade into a wooden haft. These sickles are not a chance variation of a tool-form, but have a particular significance. Their purpose is indicated by the discovery of grain together with them. It has been established that these neolithic communities cultivated wheat, beans, millet and barley.

The general character of the material culture is proof that those early inhabitants of the most fertile regions of Czechoslovakia, who founded permanent settlements, were not hunters or food-gatherers but the first farmers. They settled on the loess-uplands in the vicinity of water-courses, not by chance but because they knew that the soil in such places was suitable for cultivation. A study of the finds makes it clear that the change-over from a gathering to a productive economy, that is, to agriculture, took place in this area, as in the rest of Central Europe, about 3000 B. C. It is a great and important dividing-line in the history of the Central European communities and marks a revolutionary advance to a stage which it had taken man many tens of thousands of years to reach. These fundamental changes in the forms of economy and production, as compared with the Mesolithic Age, led the older generation of archaeologists to designate this period in which man still worked and hunted with stone implements and hunter's tools (though greatly improved), the Neolithic or New Stone Age. This period came to an end about 1800 B. C.

The Czechoslovak territory was, in the earlier stage of the Neolithic Age, part of a great European culture which stretched from Western France to the Black Sea. One of the important cultural foci was the Danube Basin. Here the farming communities developed their own distinctive material culture, known in archaeology as the culture of the Danubian people, with *spiral-meander pottery*. Witnesses to the progress made in production by these farming communities are not only the numerous stone and bone implements, but the frequent finds of pottery on their sites. It was built up by hand of fine alluvial clay mixed in some places with graphite. The earliest have the simple form of a scoop or cup shaped like an extended palm such as even nowadays one might use to drink from in case of necessity. From the pottery finds it is clear that the makers were at first satisfied with building up a special shape and with its partial baking over the flames of a fire. The original forms were thus undecorated. Later, however, decoration consisted of broad zones of incised spirals or 'volutes', combined with *pricked* designs. In addition, however, to this characteristic ornament, there was a predilection for broad bands of geometrical, zig-zag and wavy patterns. In the neighbourhood of Prague, a special group of spiral pottery has been identified known as the *Šárka type*. It is very well executed and tastefully decorated. In addition to incised patterns, there are surface tracings of spirals and triangles as well as other decorative geometrical motifs in red-coloured patterns on a dark brown or reddish brown ground. It is apparent that the potter, in all likelihood a woman, was not content merely to model a vessel, but exercised her artistic sense in order to give the vessel a more pleasing appearance. Not only the surface of the vessel, but also its shape became, in the course of time, more practical and suited to its purpose. In order to hold it more easily or even to enable it to be slung over the shoulder, it was given lugs or handles, some of which resemble animal or human heads with a hand. Relatively rarely we find line engravings of stylised human forms on the earliest farmers' pottery. On the bottom of the inside of some vessels there is engraved the symbol of a double-axe, which points to contacts between this area and the distant Aegean and Western Asian cultures. Here similar axes were used in religious rituals about 2800 B. C.

In Slovakia, the line of development was not always the same as in Bohemia and Moravia, for this part of the country broadly adjoins the Carpathian basin where characteristic cultures developed. The oldest farming communities in the western part of Slovakia shared the same material culture as that of the Czech Lands, and here, too, there are sites with typical spiral pottery. A quite distinctive group was discovered in eastern Slovakia near the Hungarian frontier. It is actually a peripheral area of the '*Bükk culture*', named after the mountain range in that region. Here these early inhabitants found rich deposits of obsidian, an ideal material for the manufacture of implements and hunting tools. This raw material was supplied to the surrounding communities and found its way far to the north and west. The sites of the farmers of the Bükk culture are both above ground and in caves. In eastern Slovakia an important site is the Domica Cave situated right on the Hungarian-Slovak frontier. In this cave, up till quite recently, the site was still in its original state and with all its material culture preserved. On the walls, paintings have been preserved executed in red colour. The inhabitants lived far from the entrance and were dependent for light on torches. They produced a very perfect type of thin-walled pottery of fine alluvial clay. The vessels are globular in shape and well baked. The surface is richly decorated, the basis of ornament being a delicate repetition pattern of spirals which sometimes gives place to incised geometrical patterns filled in with a white or yellow substance. Besides the incised motifs, there are vessels decorated with motifs painted in black on a light ground.

Into the habitat of the oldest farmers with spiral ware, there penetrated, about 2400 B. C., tribes from central Germany, a striking feature of whose material culture was pottery of hemispherical and pear shape. It is made of fine alluvial clay, the surface being divided up by a broad band of indentations forming a zig-zag or triangular pattern. On the lower part of the pear-shaped vessels there are often horn-like protuberances representing animals' and especially bulls' heads. Vessels have also been found with punctuations representing the figure of a bull, and, occasionally, there were pricked patterns representing stylised human figures.

This *stroke-ornamented* ware gained the ascendency in the environment of contemporary Czechoslovakia, and a fusion took place between its creators and the indigenous farming folk. Scarcely, however, had stability been achieved than a new and important factor intervened in the economic and social development of the territory. On the territory of what is now Hungary, as also in the Dnieper basin and in southeast Europe, an advanced farming culture arose in which the most characteristic feature was very skilfully made pottery decorated with coloured patterns. From Hungary, tribes with this style of pottery penetrated into the territory of south-west Slovakia, and especially of southern Moravia, where their settlements are most densely concentrated. Here they founded self-contained villages on hill-tops and surrounded them with ramparts and ditches. A fort of this kind was excavated at the well-known site with this Moravian *painted pottery* near the village of Hluboké Mašůvky. On the inner side of a deep ditch, two earth ramparts had been raised supported by wooden palisades. Entrance to the fort was gained by four gates. Some archaeologists see an analogy between these fortified settlements and the town plans in south-east Europe and in Western Asia, in which, at that time, craft production and trade flourished. In this region, however, that stage of development had not yet been reached and there is no attested specialized craft production. The fortified settlements with painted pottery served another purpose and had a different significance in the socio-economic structure of that time than in the previously mentioned more advanced cultural zones.

The farming folk with Moravian painted pottery used stone and bone implements and hunter's tools as did the indigenous farming communities. They were highly skilled, however, in making pottery of various shapes and sizes, which they decorated with delicately incised and coloured geometrical patterns. In the oldest stage they employed yellow and red; later a white pattern on a dark brown ground predominated. The ceramic inventory includes a very interesting bowl standing on a high, hollow pedestal. They also made rectangular lamps of clay with loops for suspension, spoons and ladles. Human and animal figures were also modelled in clay. At almost every site, and in almost every dwelling, there were complete or fragmentary female figurines of clay, in which the lower part of the trunk is strongly emphasized, while the upper part, the arms and the head, are more or less schematic. An exception is the rare find of a statuette from Hluboké Mašůvky in which the arms and hands are modelled and extended as if in benediction. A similar gesture is represented in the little clay figure from the south Moravian site near Štěpánovice.

The people with Moravian painted pottery did not live in isolation and soon they merged with the native inhabitants. A knowledge of the making of coloured pottery spread far to the west and north-west. The original painted ware gradually lost its individuality and the fusion of different ethnic units led to the rise, over a large part of Central Europe, of the so-called *Jordanówo culture*, named after the site at Jordanówo in western Poland. In the decoration of the pottery of this culture, yellow and red patterns no longer appear, but are replaced by a white pattern. A predilection is shown for perfectly smooth and polished surfaces decorated with incised geometrical ornaments filled in with white clay.

The rise and development of the Jordanówo culture at the end of the third millennium B. C. concludes the earliest stage of the New Stone Age. In addition to objects of material culture, which show a steady line of development, archaeological excavations on Czechoslovak territory have laid bare the ground plans of the dwellings of the first farming communities. The huts were rectangular and the walls were 10—40 metres long and 5—7 metres broad. In the side walls were upright posts interlaced with wicker work and plastered with yellow clay mixed with grain chaff and grass, the so-called wattle-and-daub construction. Some huts were sunk into the ground. At Střelice, near Znojmo, on the sites with Moravian painted pottery, a model of such a hut was found with a gabled roof.

From the grave finds it is evident that the earliest farming communities believed in a life after death. They buried their dead in the earth, in the contracted attitude, on their right or on their left side, the burial place being either in the settlement itself or in cemeteries on the hills near it. The folk with stroke-ornamented pottery also cremated their dead. Urns with the cremated remains of the dead were buried under barrows along with other vessels containing food and drink. Associated with the contracted burials are vessels, necklaces of marble beads, bracelets of Tertiary shells, as well as stone and bone implements and weapons. Connected with religious beliefs are the finds of figurines of bulls, goats and rams, as symbols of fertility. In the same way, the feminine figures modelled in clay, which are so common a feature at the sites of the Moravian painted ware culture, are the expression of religious beliefs and the then existing social relations. All stress the idea of fertility. This cult of the Great Mother Earth, the cult of fertility, is well attested among the farming communities of the eastern Mediterranean. The finds show, too, that woman played a very important part in such communities and was the chief factor in production. She kept the hut, worked up skins, made the pottery, sowed, reaped and milled the grain, made bread etc. Production was concentrated within the maternal *gens* in primitive communities in which there was no private ownership yet and deeper social contrasts had not yet developed.

The later stage of the Neolithic Age is full of life and movement. Domesric development is affected successively and sometimes simultaneously by outside influences. At the end of the third millenium B. C., larger and smaller ethnic groups penetrated to the territories of present-day Czechoslovakia. From the southwest, they are the people represented by the *'channelled ware'*. As the designation indicates, the vessels were decorated with sloping or vertical channelled lines. The surface of the pottery was beautifully burnished. Typical are jugs with tall cylindrical necks and a high handle. The makers of channelled ware soon gained predominance as did also their material culture. Very soon, however, there was a further triple penetration, from the Thuringian cultural area, from the Oder basin and from eastern Poland, of pastoral communities, into Bohemia, Moravia and Slovakia. They were armed with well-made stone battle axes, their culture being distinguished by the imprint of a cord pattern on the necks of their pottery. They buried their dead with great pomp in graves, with numerous food vessels and other furnishings, on hill-tops giving a wide view of the surrounding country. This pastoral folk, whose culture was considerably advanced, made an important contribution to the further economic and social development of the territory. They were not, however, the only factor to influence this development. A number of smaller ethnic groups reaching the western part of Czechoslovakia from the north and north-east also played their part. They brought with them their own distinctive material culture reflected not only in their stone and bone implements and weapons, but in their inventory of earthenware goods. These were the makers of the so-called *'globular amphorae'*, decorated on the upper part and on the cylindrical neck with lozenge-shaped pricked or grooved patterns. Beakers or drinking-cups were also introduced into the country at the end of the third millennium B. C. by foreign elements from the extensive region between the Oder and the Dnieper. At this time, archaeological finds in Bohemia, Moravia and western Slovakia provide evidence of contacts with the culture of the Laibacher Moor, from whence there came bowls on a low base, skilfully decorated with incised geometrical patterns.

All these tribes that penetrated into this area for trade or in search of new supplies of raw material for the production of stone implements and weapons, as well as the pastoral folk with corded ware, brought with them new impulses for the development of the material culture of the indigenous population distinguished by their channelled ware. It is natural that the initial isolation of individual groups was only a passing phase and that, in the course of time, all were fused to form a new whole. Thus there arose the enriched material culture of the Late Stone Age which, in archaeological literature, is known as the Chalcolithic phase. It is one of the most complex periods of Czechoslovak, and indeed, of Central European history. Sometimes, and especially in Moravia, the material culture of the Late Neolithic Age is designated the *Jevišovice culture*, after the excavated fortified settlement at Starý Zámek near Jevišovice. In reality, this culture is only a local south Moravian group within a much larger cultural area extending beyond the frontiers of Czechoslovakia into eastern Germany and into Polish territory.

The finds of the Jevišovice culture appear especially in fortified settlements established on hill-tops. The villages are surrounded by wooden palisades and, in some cases, have timbered ramparts with a filling of clay and stone. They have been discovered in many places on Czechoslovak territory. In the material culture of these settlements, the indigenous groups provide the main contribution, with additions from the north and north-east. Here, too, is apparent the share of the pastoral folk with the corded ware who, at this time, still lived as an independent ethnic group. It is thus evident from the finds that the fortified settlements were not founded by invaders for their protection, but that the reason for their existence must be sought in the economic conditions and social relations of the time. Excavations have revealed that the whole of the community's textile production was concentrated within the ramparts, as is apparent from the innumerable clay spindle whorls, clay bobbins and loom-weights hung on the ends of the warp-threads to provide the necessary tension. All the products could certainly not have been consumed in the fortified settlement and so must have been used in barter trade. Proof that barter was carried on with very distant regions are the finds of amber beads as well as of implements, weapons, and smaller objects of personal adornment made of bronze which, at this time, cannot be considered a domestic product. This trade brought the inhabitants of the fortified settlements considerable wealth and also led to the deepening of social contrasts. There was a marked increase of private ownership. The first real division of labour in the territory in the Late Neolithic Age took place after the arrival of the pastoral folk with the *corded ware*, in an environment in which husbandry was the basic economy. The pastoral form of economy was much more productive than primitive farming, while the herds belonged to individuals who then carried out their own barter transactions. Private ownership led inevitably to a gradual breaking up of the maternal *gens*. This change in the socio-economic structure is reflected in the very small number of clay female figures used as fertility charms in the archaeological finds as compared with earlier periods. The status of woman had thus considerably declined. Into the forefront of economic and social life stepped the male, who now assumed an important place in production.

At the time when these great changes were taking place, yet another group of invaders came to exercise an important influence on the economic and social structure of the communities in this territory. They were armed with daggers and bows and arrows, and their vases of fine red alluvial clay were richly decorated and in form like an inverted bell, from which is derived their name of the *Bell Beaker Folk*. Some archaeologists are of the opinion that this culture spread from the Iberian Peninsula all over Europe. New discoveries would seem, however, to point to the coast of North Africa as their focus of origin, whence they crossed to Sicily and made their way through Italy and across the eastern Alps into Central Europe and into territories here discussed. The influx of these invaders was very strong, as is testified to by the dense network of their burial-places. At first they led a nomadic existence and only later did they found their own settlements, some of which have been discovered recently, especially in Moravia. They buried their dead in cemeteries containing 20—100 graves. The skeletons are in the contracted attitude and lie on either the right or the left side, in a north-south position, and always so that they face the rising sun. Occasionally they cremated their dead. Associated with the contracted burials are food vessels, necklaces of amber beads, bronze daggers, conical bone buttons, flint arrows. On the wrist of the left arm, the archer usually has a stone plaque, concave on one side and perforated at the four corners as a wrist-guard against the recoil of the bow-string. Their material culture is, therefore, quite distinctive and easily distinguishable from the products of the native environment. Proof that the archers with the Bell Beakers were an alien group is also the fact that they have much shorter skulls than the indigenous population.

The herdsmen with the corded ware and the archers with their Beakers each maintained, for a relatively long period their characteristic, material culture and way of life. The archaeological relics leave no doubt, however, that these ethnic groups, too, at length merged with the native environment and determined the further economic, social and cultural development in the area. As result of the complex and protracted process of fusion, about 1700 B. C. there arose, enriched by new impulses, the Únětice (Aunjetitz) culture, which achieved its full flowering in the Bronze Age.

Throughout the whole Palaeolithic and Mesolithic Ages, man made his implements and weapons of stone and bone. At the close of this epoch in prehistory, however, in the Late Neolithic Age or Chalcolithic Age, occasional implements and smaller objects turn up in the settlements, made of copper or bronze. Both the archers and the pastoral folk with the corded ware possessed copper daggers. The discovery of this metal was not originally made in Central Europe at all, but in the eastern Mediterranean, in Egypt, Mesopotamia and elsewhere. From there, copper implements and weapons were brought by way of the established trade routes. It is not possible, therefore, to speak of a Copper Age in this region. Indeed, not even in the above-mentioned cultural regions was this raw material put to much practical use. It was too soft. It was discovered, however, that an admixture of tin with copper gave a much harder alloy—bronze. Bronze was introduced into the country at the beginning of the Bronze Age by foreigners. A sufficiency of tin in the Krušné Hory in Bohemia led to the rise of a metal-working industry in the native agricultural environment. This is attested by numerous finds of sandstone moulds for the casting of bronze weapons, implements and objects of adornment.

Bronze began to be used to a greater extent as a raw material about 1700 B. C. It is from this time that we may date the Bronze Age, which came to an end in the 9th century B. C. It is divided into an Early (1700—1500 B. C.), a Middle (1500—1200 B. C.) and a Late Bronze Age (1200—900 B. C.). In the course of the Bronze Age, several well-defined archaeological cultures crystallized on the territory of what is now Czechoslovakia, which do not, however, correspond in duration to the three chronological periods into which the Bronze Age falls. One of these cultures, which flourished at the end of the Early Bronze Age, is the *Únětice culture* named after the grave-finds at Únětice near Prague. The settlements and burial-places of the bearers of this culture are not confined to Czechoslovak territory, but are also to be found in the neighbouring regions. Especially large settlements are concentrated on either side of the Krušné Hory—a mountain range with considerable deposits of tin.

The people of the Únětice culture founded their settlements on uplands and slopes in the vicinity of water-courses. They set up the densest network of settlements in the prehistory of the country. Their dwellings had a rectangular ground plan, the superstructure resting on posts bearing a gabled roof. Between the posts were wicker walls daubed with yellow clay. In the vicinity of the houses, there are bell-shaped pits used as silos for the storage of grain or other agricultural products. Grain was milled on the same stone querns as in the Late Neolithic Age. Common finds in the dwellings of the people of this culture are bone daggers, awls, 'smoothers', used in the making of pottery, and needles. Spindle-whorls were made of baked clay and clay loom-weights for keeping the warp taut in weaving. The settlements also yield large quantities of fine pottery with a smooth surface, often decorated with stroke-ornamented geometrical patterns. At the end of the Early Bronze Age, the making of pottery reached a high level of technical perfection.

Our knowledge of the bronze products of the Únětice culture derives from finds in the settlements, especially grave-finds, and from so-called hoards, consisting mainly of weapons and various objects of personal adornment. Farming implements are altogether lacking. A typical weapon is a bronze dagger, triangular in plan, mounted in a wooden, bronze or even amber hilt fastened by means of rivets. The upper part of these daggers was often decorated with an engraved geometrical pattern, which is the dominant decorative motif in the Únětice culture. Besides the daggers, there was a simple flat axe-head in a horn or wooden shaft which served both as a weapon and as an implement. Objects of personal adornment were also made of bronze: earrings, several pairs of which were worn on straps across the temples, massive spiral and cuff armlets and bangles, often richly decorated with engraved patterns. High technical skill in casting is proved by the finds of bronze chains. For fastening garments, there are bronze pins of different shapes. Very characteristic are pins with a flat disk-like head decorated with a fine engraved pattern. On the neck massive neck-rings and necklaces were worn, composed of bronze spirals, of beads of amber or a vitreous substance which document trade connections between this area and the Baltic, as well as with the advanced Egyptian cultures. In the same way, gold earrings were brought from Transylvania.

The cemeteries of the people of the Únětice culture are situated on hill-tops not far from the village. They often number over 200 graves. There are, however, also smaller cemeteries. The dead were laid in oblong or oval pits, about 150 cm. below the present surface, in a contracted attitude, on an east-west axis, and on their right or left side. Sometimes there are stone slabs walling in the pits and also paving them. Some of the graves are quite spacious and contain several contracted interments. Thus the tombs were used for successive burials. When there was no more room, the remains of the previous member of the patriarchal *zadruga* were pushed to the side, along with the grave furnishings, to make way for the new interment. During the most recent excavations it has been ascertained that burials were also made in coffins hollowed out of a tree-trunk. The general burial ritual points to the belief of the people of the Únětice culture in a life after death, the deceased being furnished with at least part of the gear that had been his in his lifetime.

In the earliest stage, the people of the Únětice culture engaged in husbandry. They kept cattle, sheep, pigs and horses. For transport they made use of wooden waggons. The production of bronze as a raw material, as well as the introduction of metal-working, had a considerable effect on economic and social life. The work required considerable skill and experience, and those who had a mastery of it were real specialist-craftsmen. In sandstone moulds, or by the more advanced method of *cire-perdue* moulds, it was possible, with an adequate stock of raw material, to cast any number of tools, weapons or objects of adornment. The domestic consumption was relatively small, and so a surplus arose which could be used for barter, evidence of which are the so-called merchants' and founders' hoards hidden in the earth. These hoards, which at that time constituted real treasure, usually contained, in addition to finished goods, a large variety of old worn or broken objects, in fact, bronze scrap. Production and trade increased the amount of private property and so also intensified the social contrasts. There were now rich and poor. The greater part of the population consisted of poor farmers, for agricultural technique was still very primitive and relatively unproductive. Thus about 1500 B. C., a second great division of labour took place dividing artisans and metal-workers from workers on the land.

The proof of the existence of different social strata at that time lies in fortified settlements on hilltops, which the wealthy groups of founders and merchants erected in the middle of farming country on important

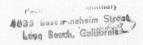

trade routes. These settlements, however, were not only centres of production and far-flung trade connexions, but, in time, came to be political and administrative centres dominating the surrounding farming area. The inhabitants of these settlements created their own material culture, which is somewhat different from the Únětice culture of the native farming population. In Moravia this culture associated with the hill-top settlements is called the *Větěřov culture*, after the important site of Větěřov near Kyjov, and, in Slovakia, the *Maďarovce culture*, after the settlement of Maďarovce near Krupina. In reality, both belong to one great cultural area including the whole of south Moravia and south-west Slovakia as far as the river Hron. It is the same territorial unit on which, in later times, various distinct material cultures arose and which, in the Early Slavonic Period, formed the economic and political core of the Great Moravian State.

From the finds at the fortified settlements at the end of the Early Bronze Age, it is evident that their inhabitants kept up lively trade and cultural relations with the advanced culture of the royal Shaft Graves of Mycenae, in Greece. Similarly finds of amber beads point to connections with the Baltic coast. Not only trade relations, however, are characteristic of this period of prehistory. The latest excavations in the northern part of Moravia and in the Oder basin, on Polish territory as well as in central Bohemia, show that several clans from south Moravia belonging to the Větěřov culture penetrated to these parts and founded here their new fortified settlements.

The economic and social development in the Únětice cultural area leading to the construction of fortified settlements on hill-tops is by no means an isolated phenomenon. A similar development is observable in the neighbouring regions and also in eastern Slovakia. Here a fortified settlement was discovered beside the village of Barca, near Košice above the river Hornád, which had been destroyed in the Early Bronze Age by a terrible fire. Almost the whole material culture has been preserved, including pottery as well as bronze and bone objects. In this settlement, too, production was concentrated and its inhabitants had lively contact with distant cultural centres. Their specialty was the production of technically very perfect pottery, richly ornamented with symmetrical knobs or bosses. The finds point to affinities with the so-called Ottoman culture, which reached eastern Slovakia from Rumania and from the western part of the Transcarpathian Ukraine.

The fortified settlements on hill-tops, which may be regarded as the earliest form of town, are also proof that the maternal *gens*, which had already begun to show signs of disintegration at the end of the Late Neolithic Age was, by the end of the Early Bronze Age, an anachronism. The extraction of tin, as well as work at the smelting furnace and founding, required a larger labour force. It is, therefore, probable that even at this time slaves were employed in production. The source of supply was the impoverished farming population or captives. There are also observable in this context the beginnings of patriarchal slavery, which assumes more definite forms as time goes on.

Over an extensive zone reaching from eastern France over southern Germany, Bavaria, southern Bohemia and along the left bank of the Danube as far east as the river Hron, there appears about 1500 B. C. and later, a very numerous folk whose chief employment was the keeping of herds and who buried their dead under barrows or tumuli. They are also referred to as the *Tumulus Folk* of the Middle Bronze Age. These people soon gained dominion of the territories in which the fortified settlements belonging to the Větěřov and Maďarovce cultures had been raised, that is, southern Moravia and south-west Slovakia. They also brought the whole of southern Bohemia under their sway and from there penetrated to the Central Bohemian plain. In the same way they advanced, in the Middle Bronze Age, about the 14th century B. C., from southern Moravia into the northern part and from there northwards into western Poland. Some offshoots of this group also reached central Bohemia from Moravia. This pastoral people naturally sought sites for their settlements where there was sufficient pasture for their herds, while in the old farming regions of Czechoslovakia there still survived the people of the original Únětice culture. Thus the two ethnic groups lived at first side by side. Only later, about 1200 B. C., did the pastoral people gain full ascendancy and determine the further economic and social development. From a pastoral economy they went over to husbandry, and also took over from the Únětice population metal-working and other forms of production.

Our knowledge of the material culture of the herdsmen of the Middle Bronze Age in this region is mainly derived from the barrow graves. These are generally located on hill-tops, and form groups numbering up to a hundred graves. Domestic sites have been less extensively excavated. The dead were buried in an extended attitude, either on the surface or in a shallow pit. Delimiting the grave was a circle of stones or of wood over which a mound of clay was erected forming the actual tumulus or barrow. This was sometimes, in its turn, surrounded by a stone kerb. In the tomb along with the body were placed the dead man's personal belongings and weapons as well as numerous vessels with food and drink. Among the barrow burials there are occasional cremations in urns. While the bronze daggers, axes, sickles, pins for fastening garments, bangles and other objects of personal adornment bear the international stamp of the time, a distinctive component of the material culture of the herdsmen of the Middle Bronze Age is their pottery, which is distinguished by its characteristic forms and technical excellence. Here we find simple and elegant jugs on a low foot, amphorae with slightly conical necks, or bowls on a notched base. The surface of the amphorae and jugs is worked up into bosses or knobs round which shallow horse-shoe grooves have been channelled. On the shoulder and body of the vessels geometrical patterns are usually incised, the interstices then being filled in with white clay.

The south Bohemian barrow culture is very similar to the finds in Moravia and Slovakia, divergences being only of interest to specialists. This similarity in the material culture of the herdsmen in south Bohemia and in the Moravio-Slovak region derives from the two groups being ethnically closely related. Both are predecessors of the earliest Celts. In their environment, too, it is evident that a wealthy group owning herds and the means of production drew apart from the rest of the population and erected fortified settlements for the protection of their property, wealth and political power. Here, too, bloody religious rites were celebrated in which human sacrifice played a part, the victims being probably captives, as is apparent from the finds of parts of human skeletons in the ditches below the fort.

The pastoral folk who, about 1400 B. C., penetrated north from southern Moravia, came to constitute in the complex process of symbiosis an important element in the rise of a large ethnical group known as the people of the *Lusatian Urnfields*. As the designation itself indicates, this folk cremated their dead and buried them in large cemeteries often numbering hundreds of graves. Sometimes these graves are covered over by barrows. This culture arose simultaneously over a large territory, and, according to the latest research, the northern half of Moravia also belonged to the original core of this culture. Towards the end of the Bronze Age, about 1000 B. C., the distribution of the Lusatian urnfields corresponds roughly to a territory lying between the Elbe and the Pripet and reaching to the Baltic Sea in the north, and including, in the south, north-east Bohemia, the northern half of Moravia and south-west Slovakia, which territory they reached last. The economic and social developments of this culture can be followed uninterruptedly up to the 5th century B. C., that is into the Early Iron Age. In this latter period, which dates from about the 9th to the 5th century B. C., two clearly distinguishable stages are to be observed in the material culture of the people of the Lusatian urnfields: an older *Silesian* and a younger *Platěnice culture*, the latter deriving its name from the gravefinds in Platěnice in the central Bohemian plain.

The most intensive investigation of settlements of the Lusatian urnfield culture has been conducted in Poland. In Czechoslovakia, large-scale excavations have so far not been carried out. Their dwellings had a rectangular or square ground plan. In addition to a spacious chamber, there was an entrance passage. In the chamber was a stone hearth, circular in shape. The construction consists of posts, with timber in between to form the walls, the spaces between the vertical logs being filled in with clay. The roof was gabled and constructed of split planks laid crosswise. Both in the villages and in the cemeteries, the most frequent finds are pottery showing an unbroken evolution from the Middle Bronze Age. In the earliest period, the ceramic inventory of the people of the Lusatian urnfields comprises types derived from the material culture of the herdsmen of the Middle Bronze Age. Later the influence of the Hallstatt style (named after the extensive cemetery in the Salzkammergut) penetrates from the south and is reflected in the preponderance of geometric motifs in the decoration of both earthenware and bronze goods. The Hallstatt culture shows a liking for the use of graphite to achieve a pleasing effect in pottery and the same predilection is observable in the ware of the people of the Lusatian urnfields.

The bronze inventory of the Lusatian culture of the Bronze Age includes bronze axes, spears, arrows, sickles, razors, bangles etc. For fastening garments, bronze pins and elaborate brooches had come into fashion, of which the main period of evolution lies between 1200 and 900 B. C. In the Early Iron Age (900—500 B. C.), the objects listed above continue to be made of bronze. New forms, however, came into use and certain objects appear made of iron. In Czechoslovakia, iron began to be used for making implements and weapons from the 7th century B. C. onwards. In the Early Iron Age, especially in the 7th and 6th centuries, the country entered into trade with the Etruscan culture of central and northern Italy, whence imports reached this region and also the territory of the Lusatian urnfields, consisting of bronze vessels, brooches and animal figurines. In the same way, vessels imitate the shapes of metal models and show a preference for black geometric designs on a yellowish brown ground.

The people of the Lusatian urnfields engaged mainly in husbandry. They cultivated wheat, barley, millet, lentils and peas. Corn was reaped with bronze and, later, with iron sickles. The grain was pounded in flat stone querns in the same way as before. In addition to farming, they kept cattle, sheep, goats, pigs and horses. Spinning and weaving was carried on quite extensively. Agricultural production was, however, as compared with the production of implements, weapons and decorative objects, strongly conservative. These differences led to the accumulation of private property in the hands of those who owned the means of production. Social differences grew more acute, the rift becoming particularly noticeable in the period of transition to the use of iron for the production of implements and weapons. Similarly, as at the end of the Early Bronze Age and during the Middle Bronze Age, there arose large fortified settlements in the agrarian environment of the Lusatian culture. On the territory of Czechoslovakia, quite a number of such sites have been discovered, but none has as yet been systematically excavated. We only know that these forts were girt with massive ramparts with timber skeletons, the interspace being filled with stone and clay. The forts were raised on important trade routes in the neighbourhood of ore deposits or other sources of raw materials. Whereas in Czechoslovakia they were situated on fairly high summits, on Polish territory the sites chosen were near lakes and water-courses. One of these monuments of the Lusatian culture dating from the Early Iron Age is the fort near Biskupin, north-west of Poznań, where the wooden constructions of log-houses and fortifications have been preserved. An interesting discovery was that of a wooden paved road leading to a massive entrance gate.

The fort was the focus of production and trade. Foreign goods of all kinds appear in the inventory, as well as large stocks of bronze weapons, implements and ornaments. There are also found bronze and iron intended as the raw material for production. It was, however, at the same time, the administrative and tribal centre for the whole territory of the people of the Lusatian urnfields, and represented a perfectly unified economic and social organisation. For a period of 800 years, this organisation resisted all attempts at agression from outside, till it at last succumbed, in the 5th and 4th centuries B. C., to the pressure of Celtic tribes coming from the west. It was the remarkable uniformity of the culture of the people of the Lusatian urnfields in the Central European environment which led scientists to investigate the problem of to what ethnic group they belonged. This has variously been claimed to be German, Illyrian and Slav. The first theory was soon abandoned, but some Polish, Soviet and also Czechoslovak archaeologists and linguists continue to regard the people of the Lusatian urnfields as Early Slavs. The majority of Czechoslovak investigators, however, do not consider this advanced culture to be of Slav origin, but as belonging to one of the ethnic groups which, in its expansion to the Vistula and further to the Dnieper, was a co-factor in the rise of the Slavs and their culture in the first millennium of our era. Nowhere, however, did the people of the Lusatian urnfields become the decisive factor determining the further course of development, but, in the process of fusion, the domestic environment always played its full part wherever this culture penetrated.

The expansion of the area of settlement of the people of the Lusatian culture is apparent from the archaeological finds of the period 1100—1000 B. C. From north-east Bohemia, a strong stream entered the territories of the Tumulus Folk in the central Bohemian plain, where fusion took place with the indigenous population, resulting in the rise of the *Knovíz culture*, named after the finds at Knovíz near Slaný. The advance of the Lusatian people did not, however, stop there, but spearheaded into south and south-west Bohemia where it gave rise to the *Milaveč culture*. Similarly, tribes belonging to the same Lusatian culture, entered south Moravia and south-west Slovakia. Here they came into contact with an advanced barrow culture, fusion with which led to the rise of the so-called *Velatice culture*, named after the grave-finds at Velatice near Brno. All the above-mentioned cultures—the Knovíz, Milaveč and Velatice— are closely related, as is to be seen both from their pottery and from their inventory of bronze, for their creators share the same ethnic base and such characteristics as were given them by the people of the Lusatian urnfields. These people were the earliest Celts, whose settlements were distributed, at the end of the Early Bronze Age and in the Iron Age, over an area reaching from the above-mentioned Moravio-Slovak region with the Velatice culture, right across Bavaria and south Germany to eastern France.

The known sites and cemeteries of the people of the Knovíz, Milaveč and Velatice cultures are relatively very numerous. Cremation was the dominating burial rite and the people of the Milaveč culture heaped barrows over the graves. The settlements are of two kinds. The one type is located on arable land, beside water-courses, and such settlements were undoubtedly inhabited by the native farming community. But in these same agricultural regions there are also fortified settlements on hill-tops, with the same material culture as those in the plains. The finds make it clear that it was at these forts that production and trade were concentrated. Here many hoards of bronze weapons, implements and ornamental objects as well as crude bronze have been found. Nor are there lacking whole necklaces of jet beads and rare objects of pure gold. It would seem that these forts were built by the people of the Lusatian urnfields, who had imposed themselves as overlords on the older indigenous communities, and who brought with them their own social organization, in which patriarchal slavery was fully developed. In these forts, too, was concentrated not only the economic but also all political and religious power. In connection with the religious rites, there are numerous finds of broken human skulls and other parts of the body which point to the rite of human sacrifice. Some investigators are even of the opinion that they are evidences of cannibalism. The forts were frequently the object of attack by neighbouring tribes. Some were taken, the fort then being destroyed and its inhabitants slaughtered with great cruelty, as has been revealed by the latest excavations of a fort of this type at Blučina in south Moravia.

Round about 750 B. C., while the Velatice culture was developing in southern Moravia and southwards to the Danube and south-west Slovakia, there appeared in this region an alien people that cremated their dead. The first extensive cremation cemetery was excavated before in the years World War I at Podolí near Brno. From it comes the term *Podolí culture* of the First Iron Age. The bringers of this culture were engaged primarily in iron smelting and forging. Their relations to the native population are, however, not yet clear to the archaeologists.

Archaeological investigation has shown that the 8th and 7th centuries witnessed a remarkable flourishing of the Knovíz culture in central Bohemia, and of the Milaveč culture in south Bohemia, as well as of the Velatice culture in the Moravio-Silesian area. The concentration of production in the hands of a small privileged group led to the accumulation of personal wealth, and the differences in economic status are also reflected in the archaeological finds. On the territory of the above-named cultures, there appear large barrows covering spacious mortuary houses of wood or stone. In central Bohemia, they are the so-called 'chieftains' graves', belonging to the Bylany culture, in which the dead are buried, in most cases in four-wheeled hearses, fully armed and equipped. Finds were made, too, of horses' yokes, richly studded with bronze nails and little plaques arranged in geometrical patterns. Very numerous also are grave-finds of horse-trappings ornamented with bronze fittings. Nor are there lacking iron and bronze horses' bits. The hearses were of wood, with wheels cased in iron tyres, and were drawn by two horses. Deposited round them were many vessels, some of which are decorated with black patterns on a light ground. Spacious chieftains' graves, with remains of hearses and horse-trappings, have also been found in south Bohemia. In the area of the Velatice culture, too, the deep social cleavages then obtaining are reflected in the rich grave assemblages beneath barrows. The first such barrow to be excavated in this country, from which numerous metal parts of horse-trappings were recovered, was the chieftain's grave at Horákov near Brno, and it has given its name to the whole culture with which it is associated.

A quite exceptional discovery that vividly illustrates the wealth and power of the ruling class in the 6th century is the burial of a tribal chieftain in Býčí skála (Bull Rock) Cave near Adamov. Here in the remote past a whole drama had been enacted, a small part of which the noted Moravian investigator, Dr J. Wankel, had the good fortune to uncover in the latter half of last century.

In the antechamber of the cave had been interred with great pomp and ceremony in a four-wheeled hearse an outstanding personality, a ruler of the people who mined and smelted iron ore in the Moravian Karst. The burial rites were solemn and bloody in accordance with the spirit of the time. Round the fragments of the hearse were found forty human skeletons—in some cases the head was missing, in others, hands and feet. A beaker made from a human skull lay there, too. Besides the human remains the finds included gold rings, bracelets and diadems and many decorated articles of bronze and iron. Against the cave walls stood bronze and pottery vessels which still contained carbonized grain—barley, wheat, rye, millet and also vetch. Charred grain was also scattered about between the vases and the skeletons. Among the finds was a bronze figure of a steer, with the Apis sign on its forehead.

There is not the smallest doubt that the richly furnished graves of the Bylany, South Bohemian and Horákov cultures contain the interments of members of a wealthy ruling group which formed a caste apart from the farming community. Graves of a similar type dating from the 7th to the 5th century are no rarity either in the territory of Bavaria, south Germany and eastern France. But also in the east, on the shores of the Black Sea inhabited by the Scythians, there are immense chieftains' barrows with tombs containing priceless treasure. The wide distribution of these graves points to the same economic and social development taking place synchronously over an extensive area. Slaves were employed in large numbers in production and provided the victims, both in religious and burial ceremonies, as is evident from the finds of skeletons or burnt bodies not only on Czechoslovak territory but also elsewhere. Domestic patriarchal slavery thus came to be an established socio-economic form in the area. It would not, however, be correct to speak of a slave order such as is known to have existed in ancient Greece or, later, on the territory of the Roman Empire.

The 'Švédův Stůl' Cave near the village of Ochoz, Moravia

The 'Kůlna' Cave near Sloup, Moravia

Inhumation of the Beaker Culture. Neratovice, near Mělník (installed by the National Museum, Prague)

Graves in the Slav cemetery at Dolní Věstonice

Slav grave with inhumation from the 9th cent. Prague, National Museum

Slav cemetery at Dolní Věstonice, Moravia. 9th cent. A. D.

Inhumation of the Roman Period. Neutonice, Prague (installed by the National Museum, Prague)

Burial of a horse in the Slav cemetery at Dolní Věstonice

The chieftains' graves, distributed over a wide territory reaching from eastern France and extending through south Germany and Bavaria right into South Bohemia, represent a ruling class derived from the Celtic peoples. In the western area of settlement of these Celts, there developed, during the 6th and 5th centuries B. C., a very advanced culture known as the *Early La Tène culture*. Strong impulses contributing to its rise and growth radiated from the advanced Italian urban cultures of the Etruscans in Italy and of Magna Grecia as transmitted through the Greek colony of Massilia (Marseilles) in southern France. From these cultural centres a rich assortment of goods reached the courts of the Celtic chiefs in the territories north of the Danube, the inventory including pottery decorated with human and animal motifs, glass bottles, gold bangles, diadems etc. Celtic artisans at first skilfully copied these imports. But the native craftsmen were not content with the mere imitation of these foreign styles. They took over certain elements and, in technically well-equipped and well-staffed workshops, created their own artistic style. The geometrical elements which had previously predominated in this area in the Early Iron Age now yielded to plant and figural decorations. The lotus leaf and palmette were the principal motifs. Important objects of personal adornment, serving at the same time to fasten the upper garment, were bronze, iron or even gold brooches of fairly large dimensions, decorated with fantastic human masks. This ornamental element appears very frequently in the Early La Tène court style.

Some of these objects, made in western workshops, also reached southern Bohemia, the most notable being ornate bronze beaked flagons. In the chieftains' graves there are also present the above-mentioned brooches with animal or human masks and bronze vessels of different kinds. The grave furnishings include disk-shaped horse's frontlets, decorated with stylised human motifs. In the ceramics inventory there appear new bottle-shaped vessels, the production of which spread from the territory of southern Bohemia to all the settled parts of this country. The earlier geometric motifs now give way to closely wound spiral coils, crosses, scrolls etc. These motifs also adorn the inside of shallow dishes. Early La Tène influences subsequently reached Moravia, though on a smaller scale.

The Early La Tène style became, in the course of time, the property of the ordinary people, but many an urge for original artistic expression was stifled by mass production. Thus arose a special domestic La Tène style, which received its designation from the finds at the Celtic arsenal of La Tène (The Shallows) discovered on Lake Neuchâtel in Switzerland. The most characteristic features of this style are bronze and iron brooches. According to the shape of these brooches, which show a distinct evolutionary line, the La Tène style has been divided into Early (400—300 B. C.), Middle (300—100 B. C.) and Late (100 B. C.) stages.

At the time when a new La Tène style was being created in the Celtic territories, southern and central Bohemia were inhabited by the Celtic Boii, who were related to the people of the Horákov culture in the Moravio-Silesian region. The Boii are mentioned in literary sources as being settled on the territory of

Czechoslovakia, further evidence of their presence here being the Latin name for this territory—Boiohemum or Bohemia. In 113 B. C., there is mention of a clash between the Germanic tribe of the Cimbri and the Celtic Boii. Side by side with the Boii, there lived in north-eastern Bohemia, the northern half of Moravia and north-west Slovakia, the older stock of the people of the Lusatian urnfields. In the 5th century, there was an influx from the Black Sea area into the southern Slovak plain of Scythians, who brought their own culture with them, but were very soon absorbed into the native agricultural population.

The Boii on the present-day territory of Czechoslovakia did not participate directly in the creation and development of the La Tène style. The bearers of this culture were the Celtic tribes living to the west of southern Bohemia. The earliest reference to the country of the Celts is preserved in the works of the geographer Herodotus living in the 5th century B. C. In a description of the land of the Scythians, with which he was well acquainted, he mentions that the Istros, by which was meant the Danube, has its source far away in the west, in the land of the Celts. Other literary sources inform us that the Celts were divided up into a large number of tribes. The most detailed account of the Celts has come down to us in the *Gallic Wars* of Julius Caesar. Valuable information about the lives of the Celtic tribes is also contained in the works of other contemporary authors such as Strabo, Pliny, Tacitus and others.

In the 5th and 4th centuries, the Celtic tribes, in the extensive territories between eastern France and southern Bohemia, started to expand in all directions. The reason for this expansion, which was militarily well organized, was economic. Production in the area of settlement had increased to such an extent that it was necessary to find both new markets and new sources of raw materials. The penetration of the Celtic tribes into other regions was thus not in the nature of a gradual colonization of these areas, but was actually a form of military occupation. The presence of Celtic tribes on Czechoslovak territories is also clearly attested by both cemeteries and dwelling sites. The cemeteries, numbering 20—100 graves, are located on hill-tops outside the settlements. The dead are interred in rectangular pits, in the extended attitude and on a north-south axis. In Slovakia, trenches have been discovered surrounding the graves, rectangular or circular in form. Male skeletons usually have a double-edged iron sword and an effective iron spear on their right-hand side. Over the body of the warrior was laid an oval wooden targe having an iron rim and a central boss. Several warriors wore a bronze or lignite armlet on the wrist or above the elbow. In addition, there are to be found, in the graves of men, women and children alike, earthenware vessels like amphorae, and dishes made on a potter's wheel. The graves of women are usually richly furnished. They have massive ornamental metal armlets on the wrists and above the elbow, as well as anklets, while in the vicinity of the trunk are ornate iron or bronze brooches used to fasten the garments in which the corpse was buried. The surface of the armlets is as a rule embellished with chased spirals and tendrils. Round their necks both men and women wore decorative neck-rings, while necklaces of gay beads are also part of the personal finery of the wealthy class. Cremations occur synchronously with inhumations and in the same cemeteries. Cremations become commoner, however, only in the first century B. C. At that time, the dead were burned on a funerary pyre, along with their full military and domestic equipment, including food vessels. The calcined bones and the remains of the different metal, glass and earthenware objects were then thrown, along with the ashes, into an oval pit, as excavations not far from Brno have shown.

Sites belonging to the La Tène culture are widely distributed and only part of them belong to the Celtic invaders who set up their courts among the local farming population. The relations between these sites is not yet clear, and only further archaeological research can throw light upon them. Economic expansion during the Celtic occupation reached its zenith in this region in the century preceding our era. During that period, fortified towns, known as *oppida*, such as those Caesar mentions, arose along important trade routes and in the neighbourhood of ore deposits. From his reports we learn, too, that the Celtic tribe of Helvetii, for instance, had 400 villages and 12 oppida. In Czechoslovakia several of fortified Celtic towns have been discovered and explored. The most important of these are the well-known forts near Stradonice and Staré Hradisko, situated on the edge of the Drahanská Vysočina beside Prostějov. The Stradonice fort was discovered at the end of the 19th century. In 1877 a find was made on the northern slope of 200 Celtic gold coins. This find of gold led to the site being considerably damaged by amateur digging. Many valuable finds have, however, passed into the keeping of the National Museum in Prague and of the Hofmuseum in Vienna. The finds were later published by the noted archaeologist, Prof. I. L. Píč, who directed the excavations — besides gold and silver coins, bronze and iron brooches, beads and bangles of yellow and blue glass, gold and bronze finger-rings with glass and enamel eyes, bronze and lignite arm-rings, bronze pendants and animal figurines, ornamental belt-buckles in the form of stylised horses' heads, bone combs, etc. Significant finds are little bronze figures representing the human form, human heads and masks which had once embellished bronze vessels or other objects. There is an immense iron inventory including, to name only some of the items, weapons and implements such as spears, arrows, saws, spurs, reins, keys, axes, sheep-shears, hatchets, sickles, iron-shod spades, etc. Bronze scales for weighing coins were among the more unusual finds. Very advanced pottery, made on a potter's wheel, is attested by numerous sherds and whole vessels, often decorated with white, yellow or red coloured patterns. The decoration is characterized by wavy lines and vertical hatching. In the clay for domestic pottery there is a strong admixture of graphite, which is characteristic of Late La Tène pottery in the region. Prof. I. L. Píč regarded the Stradonice Fort as 'the historical Marobudum', that is as the seat of the German tribe of Marcomanni. Investigation has shown, however, that at the time mention begins to be made of the Marcomanni in literary sources, that is, at the end of the 1st century B. C., the Stradonice Fort had already lost its economic and political importance and been abandoned to its fate.

Of importance equal to the Stradonice Fort at the time of the Gallic occupation of the region is the fortified settlement of Staré Hradisko in Moravia. It was known to the Bishop of the Czech Brethren, J. Blahoslav, while J. A. Comenius marked in this place on his map as '*hradisco ubi myrrha effoditur*', a fort where myrrh, that is amber, is to be found. Archaeological excavations were carried on here before the first World War, while systematic investigations were begun in 1935 and continued till 1937. A very strongly fortified settlement with an entrance gate was laid bare, built in the Celtic style. Under the ramparts of this oppidum, the ground plans of dwellings and associated buildings were disclosed, some of which were partially sunk into the ground and had gabled roofs. Other huts and buildings were framed with stakes driven into the ground, the wattle-and-daub walls being as much as 60 cm thick. As at the Stradonice oppidum, here, too, there were large finds of gold and silver coins and a rich inventory of bronze and iron goods. Many kilograms of raw amber were also found, confirming the above-mentioned reference to it made by Comenius. It would seem that this oppidum was a kind of transit station for this precious raw material.

From the investigations so far carried out, we are not yet able to form a clear picture of the mutual relations between the Celtic invaders and the native population. The historic contribution of the Celts, however, must have been above all in the field of production. Until their arrival in the area, pottery had been built up in the old primitive way by hand. The Celts, however, brought with them the potter's wheel, and, in a relatively short time, their workshop production had soon crowded the less perfect domestic production out of the market. Their arrival marked the initiation of a period of remarkable expansion in the extraction of iron and silver ores, and, in southern Bohemia, of gold-washing. The Celts were highly skilled smiths who made not only weapons but also agricultural implements and workmen's tools. Some Celtic patterns appear in the inventory of the earliest Slavs in Czechoslovakia who had previously come into contact with the Celts in the regions of the Upper Oder and Vistula. The production of more efficient agricultural implements, such as ploughs, sickles and scythes, led to improved agricultural production. Corn was no longer ground on the old saddle type of quern, but on a rotary quern which was also borrowed from the Celtic environment. At Pardubice, workshops have been discovered specializing in the production of rotary querns, as also workshops for the making of lignite bangles.

Celtic production, in which the native population supplied the labour for the heaviest work, had a considerable surplus which the local market could not absorb. Thus the fortified towns became, especially in the first century before our era, the centres of extensive trade connexions. Among themselves, the Celts used gold and silver coins, known as 'guttae iridis', as the form of payment. A large number of these minted coins have been found in southern Slovakia inscribed with the name of the Celtic chief Biatec. Coins with this inscription belong to a tribe of the Boii, who migrated to that region from Bohemia.

Julius Caesar was acquainted with only the three parts of Gaul and was probably not aware that, east of the Rhine and north of the Danube, in the so-called Hercynian Forest, there were other powerful Celtic tribes. The discovery of fortified towns and the graves of Celtic invaders led our historians to try to establish the identity of the 'Gallic' tribes who penetrated into the territory in the 4th century B. C., and, at the present time, this question is still being studied. Research workers are not unanimous, as the literary sources admit of different interpretations. It is usually assumed that in central Bohemia it was the *Volsci-Tectosages*, who, according to Caesar's account, crossed the Rhine and headed east where they established themselves in the Hercynian Forest. Some authorities claim to have identified the tribe settled in Moravia as *Cotinii*, others give this appellation to those in the Slovak Rudohoří. They were masterly smiths and, like the other Celtic tribes, remained in the region up to the 3rd century of our era. Of the *Boii* living in Bohemia and Moravia, we have already made mention.

The Celts who invaded the territories of Czechoslovakia possessed a very advanced military organization. And though there were considerable social differences between the tribal chiefs and the powerful religious cast of the Druids on the one hand and the Celtic warriors and artisans on the other, all these foreign groups showed the same tendency to exploit the native population which was mainly engaged in husbandry. Part of the population was used as forced labour in the extraction of iron and silver ore, and part in workshop production which was in the hands of the invaders. Their La Tène material culture predominated almost completely, but, towards the end of the 1st century B. C., when Celtic political power began to disintegrate, the native population revived the old traditions and began to create anew their own material culture, as is evident from the archaeological record which may be followed up to the 4th century A. D. Nonetheless, the La Tène culture of the Celtic invaders was an important contribution and substantially accelerated the economic and social development of the region.

The decline of Celtic power in the territories of Czechoslovakia and in the countries north of the Danube was only partly due to internal and mainly to outside factors. Since the 3rd century B. C., another ethnic group had been assuming increasing importance in Europe—Germans, who had their original settlements in southern Scandinavia, in Jutland and on a narrow strip of territory in northern Germany. From this focus of settlement, the Germanic tribes began to advance in an easterly and westerly direction. Some archaeologists are of the opinion that they reached northern Bohemia as early as between the 3rd and 2nd century B. C., and attribute to them the urn burials of that period. This question is not yet, however, satisfactorily settled, and Germanic settlement in this area at the time in question is improbable. Similarly, further study must be devoted to the urn burials of the Kobylis type in northern Bohemia, which archaeologists attribute to the 1st century A. D. and which are thought to belong to German bands of warriors known as *comitatus*.

Definite contact between Germanic tribes and this area took place at the turn of the millennium, that is, towards the end of the 1st century B. C. Thus it may be asserted with considerable probability that at this time the Germanic *Marcomanni* reached the territory of the old Boihaem, while another big tribe, the *Quadi*, occupied south-east Moravia and south-west Slovakia. The distribution of these tribes is still the subject of study, as no agreement has yet been reached among the authorities. Research-workers base their theories upon the reports of authors of antiquity and especially on the Greek geographer Ptolemy, who lived in Alexandria, and collected information for his comprehensive work *Germania Magna* from soldiers and merchants who had visited these regions settled by so-called barbarians. The reports not being very accurate, and not seldom conflicting, the conclusions drawn by those analysing them are also at variance.

From literary sources, too, we learn that Prince Marobud, the leader of the Marcomanni, brought a number of other Germanic tribes under his sway and created, in the region north of the Danube, a considerable military and political power on the Roman model, having himself been brought up in a Roman environment. He commanded what was a large army for those times—70,000 foot and 4,000 cavalry. This power naturally represented a threat to the Roman Empire and led to military conflicts and punitive expeditions against the Germanic tribes which ended in a victory for Rome. Marobud fled to Rome and died in 36 A. D., in Ravenna. The pressure of the 'barbarians' on the frontiers of the Roman Empire continued, however, and gave rise, in the years 166—180 A. D., to the so-called Marcomannan Wars on the territory of the Quadi in south-west Slovakia. A not inconsiderable rôle was also played in these wars, in which Marcus Aurelius finally gained the victory, by the territory of southern Moravia. The victory itself is documented in the famous Latin inscription chiselled on the rock face below Trenčín Castle, Trenčín being known at the time as the Roman garrison outpost of Laugaritium.

The Romans sought to defend their Empire against the incursions of the barbarians, and built along its northern frontier, and parallel with the right bank of the Danube, the great line of fortifications known as the *limes romanus*. Important strategic points in this defence system were the garrison stations of Vindobona (Vienna), Carnuntum, situated to the east of the village of Deutsch-Altenburg, and of Brigecia, east of Komárno, on the right bank of the Danube in Hungary. Both for strategic as well as for economic reasons, and especially in order to protect the trade routes, the Romans set up smaller garrison stations on the northern bank of the Danube, on barbarian territory, that is, in southern Slovakia and in the South Moravian plain. The most important of these was, perhaps, Mušov, situated at the confluence of the Svratka and the Dyje, in the vicinity of the Pavlov Heights, of which mention has already been made. At this station, set up in the middle of the 2nd century A. D., Roman buildings have been laid bare heated by a hot air system below the floors. The bricks bear the stamp of the Xth Legion, whose headquarters were in Vindobona. The Mušov garrison outpost has been identified with the settlement of Phaelicia mentioned by Ptolemy. North of Mušov, at the castle of Staré Zámky by Brno, the remains of Roman buildings have also been discovered. This is possibly the old settlement of Meliodunon, which is cited as lying north of Phaelicia. Other Roman stations have been identified near Stupava, west of Bratislava, at Děvín Castle, above the junction of the Morava with the Danube, and also in the Bratislava area itself. The easternmost station is Kelemancia, situated on the left bank of the Danube opposite Brigecia.

Trading relations between the Roman Empire and the territories of present-day Czechoslovakia are also documented by finds of products from Roman workshops, a typical example of which is *terra sigillata* pottery made of fine brilliant red clay. Vessels made of terra sigillata were not wheel-thrown, but pressed into moulds. The surface is usually decorated with human, animal and plant motifs in relief. Terra sigillata ceramics were first produced in the Italian workshops; later production was taken over by workshops in the Rhine Basin and also in the territory of present-day Bavaria. Of similarly high quality were the so-called *terra nigra* products of which sherds have also been found in the region. Finds made here of bronze and glass vessels are evidence of connexions with the Roman Empire. Numerous stray finds, but also whole collections of gold, silver and copper Roman coins minted in the first four centuries of our era, are further conclusive proof of the presence of Roman soldiers, especially in Slovakia and southern Moravia, as well as of active trading relations between the two groups. The native population, however, did not use coins as currency, but as objects of adornment. Perforated Roman coins were thus often worn as pendants.

It has been established that, between the 1st and 4th centuries A. D., many settlements grew up on Czechoslovak territory in the neighbourhood of water-courses. The houses were mostly built on the natural surface, and so the original ground plans have not been preserved. Some few houses were, however, partly sunk into the ground, usually rectangular in shape, the walls being supported by stakes and covered with a gabled roof. Some huts having a circular ground plan have also been brought to light of the same type as is represented on the famous Victory Column of Marcus Aurelius in Rome. Inside and in the vicinity of both rectangular and circular houses, there are pear- or cauldron-shaped pits serving for the storage of grain or other supplies. Relatively little attention has been paid so far to the investigation of these sites from Roman times, but, even so, the research carried out would seem to point to the decay of the greater part of these sites during the 2nd and at the beginning of the 3rd century A. D., while a minority survived in certain parts of the country up to the beginning of the 4th century.

The dead were buried in cemeteries situated on hill-tops in the neighbourhood of the village. From the 1st up to the beginning of the 4th century A. D., the predominant burial rite was cremation. Urns with the ashes of the deceased, weapons and objects of personal adornment were laid in shallow graves not far beneath the present-day surface. Most of these cemeteries have in consequence been destroyed by deep ploughing. As a rule, such a cemetery contained 100—200 graves, but there are also much larger burial-places. The urn graves contain iron spears, knives, sheep-shears, pincers and bronze, iron or silver brooches. In the first-century graves there are also remains of bronze and glass vessels melted or vitrified by fire, while gay beads made of some vitreous substance are also among the grave-finds. In the 3rd century, the metal and also the other finds from the urn graves are relatively rare. At the beginning of the 1st century A. D., extended inhumation burials make their appearance in the urnfields. They are on a north-south axis — a typical Celtic feature — and their greatest concentration is in the central Bohemian plain. They are also usually richly furnished with bronze vessels made in Italian workshops. Insofar as these inhumation graves occur in the Moravian urnfields, they are decidedly poor. In Bohemia, on the other hand, they seem to have belonged to a wealthy Celtic oligarchy. A strong Celtic tradition is also apparent in the pottery of the Pichora stage, which was mostly built up by hand. In the 3rd century, especially in the territories of Moravia and Slovakia, vessels appear skilfully thrown on the potter's wheel. A fine grey clay purged of impurities was used for making this pottery. The majority of the vases are decorated with scrolls filled in with vertical hatching. Not far from Brno, near Jiříkovice, was found a kiln for the firing of this pottery, produced here on a large scale by experienced craftsmen and supplied to a wide area. Some authorities hold the view that the producers were members of the Celtic tribe of the Cotinii, which maintained itself in Moravia up to the 3rd century A. D. These workshops were, however, more probably connected with the Black Sea culture.

Finds from sites of the Roman period belong to the so-called *Dobřichov culture*, after the site in central Bohemia where the urnfields at Pichora and Třebická have been excavated. The urn burials at Pichora date from the 1st and 2nd centuries A. D., whereas those at Třebická may be attributed to the 3rd and the beginning of the 4th century. Today, it is usual to divide the Dobřichov culture into an early (0—150 A. D.), middle (150—270 A. D.) and late (end of the 3rd and beginning of the 4th century) period. This division is not, however, definitive. At the time when settlements and cemeteries associated with the Dobřichov stage (1st—2nd century) of material culture are attested for Bohemia, Moravia and Slovakia, there lived, in the hilly regions extending from the east of Moravia to Poprad in Slovakia, a people who raised fortified settlements on inaccessible hill-tops. The finds are described as belonging to the *Púchov culture* and show strong traces of La Tène influence.

It is assumed that these fortified villages with Púchov culture most probably belonged to the Celtic tribes who, under pressure from Germanic and Slav tribes, retreated to the above-mentioned hilly country.

In the 3rd and 4th centuries, the archaeological finds in the northern half of Moravia point to affinities with the central basin of the Elbe. So, for instance, the extensive cemetery in Kostelec, in the Haná district, is attributed to the German tribe of the Buri. In north-west Bohemia, there is evidence, at this time, of close contacts with the Hassleben environment and with artisan and craft workshops in Thuringia. These contacts play an important part in the rise of the *Vinařice culture* which, however, does not develop fully till the 5th century. Moravia and Slovakia, on the other hand, take over, in the course of their economic and cultural development at the end of the 3rd, and throughout the 4th century A. D., impulses from the cultural stream which reached these parts from the region of ancient craft workshops on the northern shores of the Black Sea. Frequent raids by the local inhabitants and by the armed bands of the ruling German oligarchy from the Moravian-Slovak region north of the Danube into the territories of the Roman Empire led to the accumulation of considerable wealth by the participants in these raiding excursions who also began to adopt various Roman customs which they introduced into the local complex. Thus a new religious cult and new burial rites came into fashion in the territories of Czechoslovakia. Social contrasts were sharpened. The wealthy were buried in spacious graves, unburned, and surrounded by a great treasure of gold and silver jewellery, ornaments, implements, weapons, as well as glass, bronze, silver and gold vessels. Similarly rich graves dating from the 3rd and the first half of the 4th century have been discovered in several places on Slovak territory, among the most interesting of which are the graves at Stráže near Piešťany.

Only a very small proportion of the settlements from the first four centuries A. D. belonged to the German invaders, while the rest must be attributed to an earlier farming stock intermixed with Celtic artisans. Archaeological investigation has established that these sites decayed or were abandoned at the end of the 3rd century and at the beginning of the 4th, when the thread of evolution breaks off. This historic fact has an explanation.

The internal decay of the Roman Empire and the break-up of the slave economy were accelerated by the incursions from the upper Danube of the 'Barbarians'. The frontier on the Danube, once so firm and strong, gave way, so that in the second half of the 4th and at the beginning of the 5th century, that is, just when the so-called Migration of Peoples began, several ethnic groups, large and small, that had advanced from the north and east, took possession of the rich province of Pannonia in what is now western Hungary. From here they directed their attacks against the very heart of the Empire—against Italy itself. An important factor in the complicated events of this extremely unsettled period of European history was presented by the earliest Slavs.

THE BEGINNINGS AND EARLY STAGES OF SLAVONIC DEVELOPMENT

As in the past, so also at the present time, Czechoslovak archaeologists are devoting a great deal of attention to questions connected with the earliest Slavonic settlement and the development of a Slavonic material and spiritual culture in this part of Central Europe. In seeking a solution to these complex problems, they try to avoid all nationalist or chauvinist tendencies; rather is it their endeavour to establish, on the basis of proper scientific research, when Slavs first appeared on the territory of present-day Czechoslovakia and what their contribution is to the economic and social history of Central Europe. A solution of these questions is all the more urgent as, in the work of certain historians and archaeologists, treating of the historic process which ran its course on Czechoslovak territory in the first millennium of our era, there is still evidence of divergent tendencies and interpretations. In some such pseudo-scientific works we may read, for instance, that the Slavonic settlement of Czechoslovakia took place under pressure from the Avars, thus relatively late, or that Slavonic farming communities were incapable of independently forming larger political or social groups and that they took over much of their material and spiritual culture from the West. In this way, a persistent attempt is made—and especially on the basis of archaeological finds—to justify the function of the Border Lands, the so-called Sudeten, which, they claim, has been since the earliest times a region of mixed ethnical groups.

The outstanding antiquaries, P. J. Šafařík, and his successor, L. Niederle, showed in their compendious scientific works, which they entitled *Slavonic Antiquities*, how rich the history of the Slavs is and what an important part they played in the economic, social and cultural development of the European peoples. L. Niederle was not content with a mere analysis of the extant literary sources, but also took into consideration the archaeological relics from the early Slavonic settlements and cemeteries. A study of the material led him to the conclusion that the original home of the Slavs lay between the Vistula and the Dnieper north of the Carpathians, that is, where the earliest literary sources locate the great tribe of the Neuri, as early as in the 5th century B. C., and later, in the 1st and 2nd century A. D., the large ethnic group of the Wends along the banks of the Vistula. Today there is no longer any doubt but that these two national groups belonged to the Slav family of peoples. Indeed, the designation 'Wends' has survived as an appellation for Slavs in the German language up to this day. From this original home of the Slavs, Slav tribes began, according to Niederle, at the end of the 2nd century A. D. to move out in all directions, and thus part of them also reached the territories of present-day Czechoslovakia.

Even at the time when Niederle wrote his *Slavonic Antiquities*, differing views were held as to the origin of the Slavs by archaeologists, historians and linguists, both in Czechoslovakia and, especially, in Poland. Nor is there complete unanimity even today. Most Czech research-workers uphold in the main Niederle's original theory, but there are also supporters of a theory of the autochthonous rise of the Slavs on Czechoslovakian territory and in Central Europe generally. The outstanding Polish authority on linguistics,

Prof. Lehr Spławiński, would locate the core of the Slavonic peoples in the territory between the Oder and the Vistula, from which, as he believes, there was a general expansion, in the 5th century B. C., in all directions. Some Russian archaeologists, notably the well-known authority, P. N. Tretyakov, as well as other scholars, does not endorse the conclusions reached by Niederle, but claims an autochthonous development for the eastern Slavonic tribes on the extensive territories in which they are to be found at the end of the first millennium A. D.

The decisive factor in the solution of the problem of the origin of the Slavs and their earliest settlements in Czechoslovakia, as well as for the tracing of their economic and social development in the first ten centuries of our era, is archaeological investigation, able to provide the significant data from which a true historical picture can be built up. Ever since the inception of prehistory as a science, Slav archaeologists have directed their investigations towards discovering settlements and cemeteries which could be attributed to the oldest Slavs in the European environment. Much study has been devoted to the bringers of the culture of the Lusatian urnfields with which the reader is already acquainted. Niederle and his contemporaries regarded it as Slavonic. Later, however, he himself abandoned this theory on the grounds that there was not sufficient evidence to prove genetic connexions with the known material culture of the Slavonic settlements and cemeteries of the 9th and 10th centuries. The Lusatian urnfields are considered to be Slavonic above all by Polish archaeologists, especially by the Poznań school led by Prof. J. Kostrzewski. Among Czech archaeologists, it is the school of Prof. J. Filip that most closely approaches the Poznań school in its conclusions, Prof. Filip having adduced no less than 38 reasons in support of his attribution of the Lusatian urnfields to Slavs, giving it as his opinion that the people settled on the territories of what is now Czechoslovakia are to be regarded as the predecessors of the later Slavs. But while, today, there are still historians who uphold the opinion that this distinctive archaeological culture is Slavonic, the majority of research-workers in this field take the view that it is not Slavonic, but one of the important constituents in the rise of a Slavonic culture in the course of the Slav advance towards the Vistula and the Dnieper. In this region, however, the Lusatian culture did not determine the further development, in which the main historic role was played by the older farming stock as was the case in all those territories into which the people of the Lusatian urnfields penetrated.

The Lusatian culture will no doubt continue to be the subject of further scientific study. In order, however, to establish the earliest date of Slavonic settlement on Czechoslovak territory, a number of archaeologists decided to work backwards, step by step, from the known to the unknown instead of making a leap into prehistory. Niederle stated frankly that Slav settlements and cemeteries of earlier than the 9th century are not known. Here and there urn graves were discovered in which the ashes of the defunct had been placed in vessels very similar to the pottery with which we are familiar from grave-finds of the 9th and 10th centuries. There was, however, no firm basis for the dating of these objects as there were no associated grave-goods of metal or other objects. The age of these graves was thus determined solely on the basis of the typology of the pottery and the conclusion reached that they belong to the 7th and 8th centuries of our era.

Special attention has been paid by archaeologists to a group of undecorated urns built up by hand which are to be found along with vessels decorated with wavy lines. These graves with undecorated urns have been persistently attributed to a German culture. Dr. I. Borkovský has proved by detailed study that, in reality, these urns represent the earliest Slavonic pottery in Central Europe. He classified them as the *Prague type* and attributed them to the 4th and 5th centuries A. D. The evolutionary continuity of the earliest Slavonic culture has been established especially by Moravian and Slovak finds during the last decade. Whole cemeteries have been discovered in which, alongside undecorated pottery of the Prague type, there are vessels of more advanced shapes decorated with characteristic Slavonic wavy-line motifs such as we come across on the extensive territories of West, East and South Slavs throughout the whole second half of the first millennium A. D. At the present time, a cemetery of the oldest Slavs in Czechoslovakia is being excavated beside the village of Přítluky in southern Moravia, on the banks of the Dyje. Here, over 600 urn graves have been laid bare, in which grave-finds of metal objects and Roman brooches date the first burials as taking place during the 4th century. This cemetery is thus one of the largest and earliest monuments of Slavonic culture not only on Czechoslovak territory, but in the territories of the Western Slavs in general, and is, at the same time, a proof of dense settlement in one of those border zones in connexion with which scientific research is carrying out a basic correction of subjective theories which would seek to establish here the existence at this period of German settlements.

A dense network of Slavonic settlements, in existence during the 4th and 5th centuries, is attested also in other parts of Czechoslovakia. It has been proved, too, that the original settlements of the non-Slavonic farming communities, among which remnants of Celtic tribes survived, lost their significance during the 3rd and at the beginning of the 4th century. The reason for their decline is to be sought in the fact that, from the end of the 2nd century, an infiltration had been going on of Slavonic agricultural and pastoral tribes into Czechoslovak territory from the region of the upper courses of the Oder and Vistula. There the great tribe of the Lugii are known to have settled and founded their own villages. In the process of symbiosis with the native environment, they became, in all respects, the dominating constituent, and determined, from the 4th and 5th centuries, the further economic and social development in the territories of present-day Czechoslovakia, not excepting the Border Lands. A distinctive feature of the material culture of the earliest Slavs is the undecorated pottery of the Prague type to which reference has already been made and which was the product of domestic skill and creative expression.

Archaeological exploration of the oldest Slavonic settlements and cemeteries in Czechoslovakia is so far only in its beginnings, and does not permit of any definitive conclusions regarding the economic and social development. The siting of the settlements points to agriculture and the keeping of herds as being the main occupation of the Slavonic people. They cultivated grain, millet and poppies for poppy seed, and reared horses, cattle, goats, pigs and sheep. Poultry, too, was abundant. Pottery, textiles and the other necessities of daily existence were produced between the 3rd and 7th centuries in the individual Slavonic households. There was, however, one branch of production which was not carried on within the area of the farming settlement. It was the extraction of iron ore and the working of the metal. This was the work of specialists who lived in the immediate vicinity of the deposits, as is evident from finds in urn graves with pottery of the Prague type in the ferriferous areas of the Moravian Karst where normal farming settlements never occur.

The most important rôle in the lives of the earliest Slavonic inhabitants of the area was played by the soil. The basis of the social structure was the patriarchal extended family or *zádruga*. Its existence is confirmed by the excavation of urn graves under barrows at the above-mentioned cemetery at Přítluky in southern Moravia. Here, up to 24 graves were found beneath one barrow. These could not have belonged to one monogamous family, but only to a larger social unit. The original organisation by families was, therefore, breaking up among the Slavs of the 4th and 5th centuries, and the patriarchal *zádruga* was only a transi-

43

tional socio-economic unit out of which there arose, in the course of further economic development, the well-known Slav farming community or *občina* of free farmers and their families living in their own houses and farming holdings allotted to them from the common property of the community.

During the 5th and 6th centuries, the Slavs on Czechoslovakian territory came into contact with the German armed bands. These are represented in the archaeological record by smaller cemeteries in which the dead were buried burnt in deep pits having an east-west orientation. Most of these graves were robbed in early times, for they usually contained valuable grave-goods, as is evident from the graves at Blučina and at Smolín in southern Moravia. At Blučina, the grave of a tribal chief was discovered, on the right of the skeleton being a sword with a gold-worked hilt and on the left a large iron knife, a so-called scramasax, the sheath of which had a massive gold mount studded at the top with almandines. On the wrist of the right hand was a massive gold armlet—at that time a symbol of authority—weighing almost a quarter of a kilogram. Bits of gold harness and various kinds of metal work, also inlaid with almandines, were found here, along with a wooden bucket with silver-work hoops, fragments of three slim glass goblets, a quiver with iron arrows and bits of a bow, a Late Roman brooch and other objects. Similarly, in a woman's grave at Smolín, there was a great treasure of feminine ornaments, including silver brooches and gold earrings, besides numerous coloured and amber beads. Among the outstanding monuments witnessing to the existence of foreign armed bands on Czechoslovak territory, at a time when there was continuous Slav settlement, is the great barrow grave of Žuráň, situated east of Brno. In an immense stone construction raised over a round base having a diameter of about 60 metres, two spacious graves were laid bare, on the edges of which are traces of a wooden construction. Both had been robbed. In one were the bones of several horses, in the other the skeletal remains of a woman of about 40 and gold thread from her garments, along with the remains of a conical pyxis for jewels, made of ivory and decorated with Early Christian scenes in relief. The finds probably belong to the end of the 5th century.

The furniture of the graves with unburnt skeletons shows that a number of them are connected with the penetration of West German armed bands or tribes. In north-west Bohemia, very close connexions are apparent with the distinctive culture of German Thuringia. Several cemeteries belonging to the first half of the 6th century A. D., discovered in central Moravia, are attributed to the Longobardi. The majority of cemeteries in Moravia and Slovakia dating from the 5th century of our era have clear affiliations, as regards their material culture, with the area of famous workshops on the northern shore of the Black Sea. As to determining to what ethical groups these graves belong, they might be hypothetically attributed to Ostrogoths or Alani. A definitive identification of the nationality of these graves dating from the period of the Migration of Peoples is problematic, for almost all of them have their individual character, nor is their inventory uniform either chronologically or in respect of provenance. Finds of artificially deformed women's heads are also proof that the armed bands whose cemeteries appear on Slavonic territory were in contact with the Black Sea regions. This custom was widespread in the countries bordering on the Black Sea in the 5th century. Literary sources mention that people with deformed skulls were called *macrocephali*.

As already stated, continuous Slav settlement of the territories of Czechoslovakia in the 5th and 6th centuries is clearly attested. These centuries were a period of considerable unrest in the European environment. It is known as the time of the Migration of Peoples, in which the German tribes and armed bands played a considerable rôle. Being well equipped with heavy weapons such as iron swords, spears and axes, they temporarily subdued the native populations and lived off native resources. These bands never founded permanent settlements in the area which could be looked upon as a continuation of the settlement by the Quadi or Marcomanni. Only relatively small cemeteries have been found, while domestic sites are unknown. Thus they must either have left the Slovak farming areas or been completely absorbed into them.

The foreign armed bands were not, however, the only factor affecting the economic and social development of the Slav people in Czechoslovakia. From the second half of the 6th century, numerous raiding expeditions of Avar horsemen penetrated into Slovakia from the territory of present-day Hungary, which they had reached from the Black Sea. The Slavs settled on the northern banks of the Danube did not remain passive in face of these hostile incursions and, in the first half of the 7th century, offered active resistance. Under the leadership of the historic Prince Samo, the first larger military alliance of Slavs against the Avars was formed, and the Avars suffered a crushing defeat. The central core of the large Samo's state was the south Moravian plain on the lower courses of the Morava and the Dyje. No sooner, however, was the Avar threat averted than the bands of this alliance were loosened and local princes again ruled over their tribal domains.

As the archaeological record shows, the Avar raids continued in southern Moravia and southern Slovakia throughout the whole of the 8th century, proof being the numerous graves of Avar-Slavonic cemeteries in which Avar horsemen are buried along with Slav farmers and artisans. A characteristic feature of these mixed cemeteries are finds of bronze metalwork decorated with plant, animal and human motifs, the originals of which had been brought by the Avars from the Black Sea regions. In the new environment of the Carpathian Basin, these objects, decorating saddles and horse-trappings as well as men's leather belts, continue to be turned out with characteristic variations. An important share in this production fell to the Slav metallurgical centres, and it would seem that some of them were located in southern Moravia and in southern Slovakia.

At the end of the 8th century, Charlemagne's forces broke the power of the Avars in what is now Hungary, while those that lived in the Slav territories north of the Danube were gradually assimilated. With the fall of the Avar power, the production of decorative metal work declined and finally lapsed into oblivion. On the other hand, in the 7th, and especially throughout the 8th and at the beginning of the 9th century, Slav material culture begins to unfold in full measure on Czechoslovak territory. There was a flowering of all branches of craft production, which reached its height in the second half of the 9th century. An expanding economy and the growth of private property are reflected in the socio-economic structure of the time. The tribal chiefs had the greater part of craft and agricultural production in their hands. In case of labour shortage, slaves were employed, recruited from the ranks of the impoverished native population or from the captives taken in intertribal warfare. Such labour was, however, not sufficiently productive, and so other ways were sought to provide the man-power necessary for cultivating large holdings. Free Slav farmers were forced to do the work, so that gradually they came to form a villein class dependent on the tribal chiefs and on their military following. Thus, at the end of the 8th and the beginning of the 9th century A. D., there arose in Czechoslovakia mutually opposed classes, and the economic and social preconditions were created for the birth of a super-tribal organisation in the form of the Great Moravian State. It is not then mere chance that, at the Frankfurt Synod in 822, envoys were present not of the individual Moravian tribes but of the Moravians. Indeed, Moravia was at that time united in a Great Moravian Feudal State, in which there was a ruling oligarchy of Mojmírs on the one hand and masses of unfree land workers and artisans on the other.

The tribal chiefs had earlier raised strong forts to protect their power and wealth and a larger number of such strongholds are scattered over the territory. On the rise of the Great Moravian State, these forts lost their importance and were absorbed into the larger state organisation. In the 9th century, and especially in the second half of the century, the same fate overtook other fortified Slavonic villages in which all production in certain regions of the Great Moravian State was concentrated as well as all trade. One of these Slav settlements numbering over 5,000 inhabitants is Veligrad, mentioned in literary sources and situated on the territory of Staré Město, on the right bank of the Morava. Excavations have brought to light up to 2,000 Slav graves as well as the foundations of two walled churches. Another church has recently been laid bare not far from Staré Město near the village of Modrá. These finds are evidence of the advanced culture of the early Moravians at the time of the Great Moravian State, which had close relations with Byzantium. Further proof is the presence on this territory of two eminent Christian missionaries—Cyril and Methodius, who preached the Gospel of Christ to the Moravians in the Slavonic tongue. Beside the churches, very rich graves of Slav women were found, with rich grave-furniture including gold and silver ornaments. The men's graves yielded numerous iron spears, axes and swords. A large amount of pottery has also been discovered, including two-handled amphorae and flat flasks. Proof of skilled metal-work and cooperage are wooden metal-mounted buckets. All the finds show the maturity of the Early Moravian craftsmen who, in many respects, created an altogether distinctive culture. Originally it was thought that the rich gold and silver objects of personal adornment were from Byzantine workshops. It has been proved, however, that no ornaments of these designs and execution are to be found anywhere in the Byzantine region. Thus the finds on the Staré Město site must be regarded as the domestic products of Slav goldsmiths, a conclusion corroborated by finds of fragments of gold objects (scrap) and unworked gold in the graves.

Large centres such as that of Veligrad were not destroyed on the rise of the Great Moravian State at the beginning of the 10th century, it being possible to follow their economic development up to the end of the 10th century. At this time of economic and social confusion they were abandoned, and the centres of political power were transferred to Bohemia, to the territory of the Přemyslides. Here the tribal chiefs maintained their power much longer than in Moravia or Slovakia. The 10th century still witnessed the struggle waged between the two powerful clans of the Přemyslides and the Slávníks, each of which held dominion over roughly half of Bohemia. This struggle for power culminated in 955 with the almost complete extermination of the Slávníks. It was at this point that a supertribal organisation began to take shape—the Czech feudal state, with its centre at Prague Castle, which, in the course of the 11th century and later, acquired political dominion over Moravia, while Slovakia came more and more under the oppressive yoke of Magyar power.

It has not been possible here to give the reader more than a cursory view of the complex process of economic and social development on the territory of Czechoslovakia that can be pieced together from the archaeological record. From our account it is clear that, in connexion with certain periods of prehistory, much still remains obscure owing to the inadequacy of the archaeological material so far discovered. Many a secret still lies buried in the earth and many a clue to an unsolved problem. Yet the wealth of monuments and relics which archaeology has brought to light and classified are irrefutable evidence of the work, thought and artistic expression of those numberless generations who, since the dawn of history, have carried human progress forward step by step. In its manifestations, in its production, is clearly reflected man's general economic and social development and its conformity to its own evolutionary laws. Sometimes the historic process unfolded more quickly, sometimes more slowly, but it never went back, never came to a standstill, but always went steadily forwards. In obedience to the laws of social evolution, the first socio-economic formation of primitive communism decayed and was replaced by a new and more progressive structure.

In discussing the cultural and economic history of the area in Slav and pre-Slav times, so-called external influences are often metioned. Such external influences are usually over-estimated. They cannot however be ignored. Let us just recall how even in the New Stone Age the area had already come in contact with the cultural provinces of the Mediterranean and of Asia Minor. At the end of this period of prehistory, fresh impetus was given to economic expansion in the Czech Lands and Slovakia by the 'chalcolithic' herdsmen with corded ware who invaded the modern Czechoslovakia from Thuringia, Poland and the Ukraine. So, too, did the archers of the Bell Beaker culture whose cradle is to be sought in North Africa. During the Bronze Age Moravia and Slovakia maintained active intercourse with the Carpathian basin, while in the Iron Age the area came into economic and cultural contact with the Hallstatt culture, whose centre lay in the Austrian Alps. No less significant for further progress in Bohemia and Moravia were the Celts who advanced from the west. In Slovakia they encountered the Scythians who brought a highly developed culture from the Black Sea steppes.

Czechoslovakia's contacts with the Roman Empire, lasting over 400 years, were of course not without importance for its economic and cultural development. Late Roman workshops existed in the 5th century in western Hungary on the territory of ancient Pannonia whither Slav tribes spread from southern Moravia and Slovakia. These tribes adopted many elements of late Roman culture, notably the production of iron agricultural implements and weapons, the manufacture of gold, silver and bronze ornaments and a superior ceramic technique.

In connexion with the question of the Great Moravian State, whose centre lay on the Lower Morava and the Dyje, it is possible to deduce relations with the Byzantine world in the light of excavations in Pannonia. These relations were particularly close in the time of Prince Rostislav and were likewise connected with the mission of Cyril and Methodius. The Slav people in our lands between the 5th and 9th centuries already knew how to bring into harmony all external impulses and created for themselves a material and spiritual culture on the basis of their own distinctive ideas. Hence the Great Moravian State, as well as the Czech Feudal State, is a product of economic processes on the spot.

ECONOMIC AND SOCIAL DEVELOPMENT IN CZECHOSLOVAK TERRITORY UP TO FEUDALISM

Years	Socio-economic structure		Production		Archaeological culture	Chronology	Climate	Years
1 000	Feudalism		Specialization of trades		Slavonic	Czech Feudal State		1 000
800	Pre-feudal Period	Patriarchy	Agriculture	productive		Great Moravian Empire		800
500	Slavonic *občina*					Slavs and Avars	cool and damp (Sub-Atlantic)	500
					*Indigenous culture of native inhabitants with admixture of Roman influence	Earliest Slavs in Czecho-slovakia		
0	Military dictatorship		Potter's wheel / Rotating quern			Czechoslovak territories in contact with the Roman Empire		0
500	Patriarchal slave-ownership		Iron ore-founding / Iron-working		La Tène — Finds in Býčí Skála by Adamov — Bylany, Horákov, Podolí, Knovíz-Milaveč-Velatice	Celts		500
1 000						Hallstatt	warm and damp Atlantic	1 000
2 000			Bronze-casting / Bronze-working		Pastoral folk of the South Bohemian and Danubian barrows, Únětice, North Pannonian, Corded ware, Bell Beaker, Channelled ware, Jevišovice, Moravian painted ware, Jordanov	Bronze Age	Sub-Boreal	2 000
3 000			Spinning / Stock-rearing		Stroke-ornamented ware, Spiral pottery	Late Stone Age (Chalcolithic) / New Stone Age (Neolithic)	warm and dry Boreal	3 000
			Oldest farmers					
10 000	Primitive	Matriarchy	Hunters of small game and fishers	unproductive	Tardenoisean	Middle Stone Age (Mesolithic)		10 000
20 000					Magdalenian, Gravettian, Aurignacian		Last Ice Age	20 000
75 000	communities		Reindeer-hunters / Mammoth-hunters		Mousterian	Old Stone Age (Palaeolithic)		75 000
			Bear-hunters		Acheulean, Abbevillean			
250 000								250 000

(Archaeological culture human-type labels: Lusatian Urnfields; Neanderthaler; Cro-Magnon Man)

ILLUSTRATIONS

PALAEOLITHIC OR OLD STONE AGE

3. Pendant with large, single knob · Mammoth bone · Aurignacian culture · Předmostí (Přerov District) · Dimensions: 10 × 4 × 1 cm · Moravian Museum, Brno

2. Pregnant woman seated (Venus) · Mammoth's phalanx · Aurignacian culture · Height: 14 cm · Předmostí (Přerov District) · Moravian Museum, Brno   ←

1. Stylised female figure engraved on a mammoth's tusk · Aurignacian culture · Length: 31.0 cm · Předmostí (Přerov District) · Moravian Museum, Brno   ·/. ←

4. Statuette of a mammoth · Mammoth bone
· Aurignacian · Height: 11.7 cm · Předmostí
(Přerov District) · Moravian Museum, Brno

5. Reconstruction of the mammoth statuette from pl. 4.

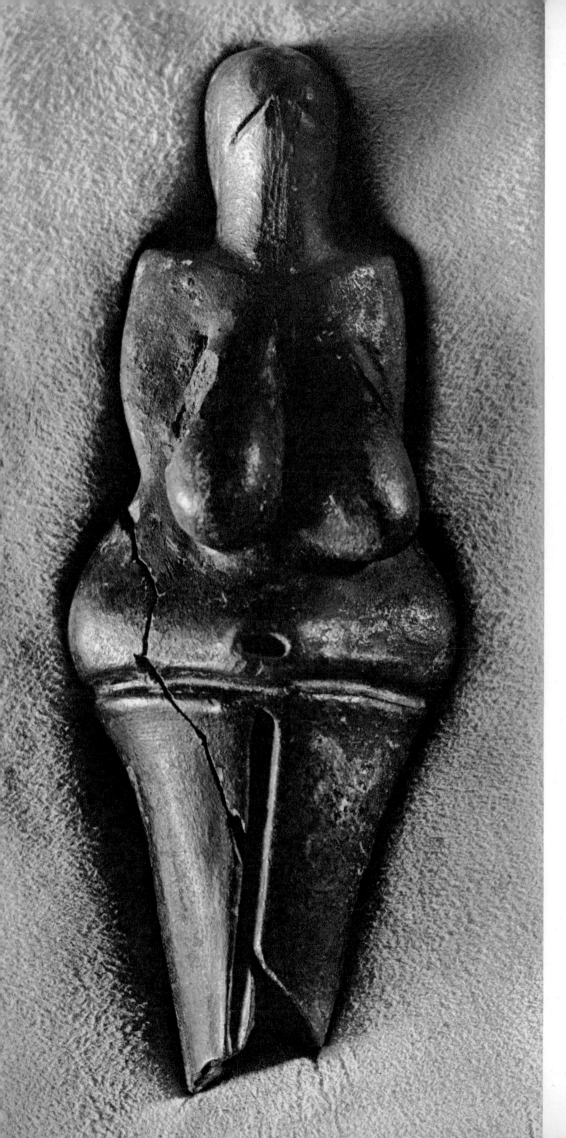

6. +7. Female statuette · The Věstonice Venus I. · Baked clay · Upper
Aurignacian (Gravettian) · Height:
11.5 cm · Dolní Věstonice (Mikulov
District) · Moravian Museum, Brno

I. Zoomorphic vessel and model of animal ·
Brodzany (Partizánské District), Slovakia ·
Lengyel Culture · Pottery · Max. length:
8.0 cm; max. length of animal: 4.0 cm ·
Museum in Bojnice (Prievidza District)

8. Stylised female figures · Mammoth bone ·
Upper Aurignacian (Gravettian) · Height:
8.6 cm; 8.7 cm · Dolní Věstonice (Mikulov
District) · Moravian Museum, Brno   ←

9. Female torso · Haematite · Upper Aurignacian (Gravettian) · Height: 5.0 cm · Ostra-
va-Petřkovice · Czechoslovak Academy of
Sciences, Archaeological Institute, Brno

10. Male statuette · Mammoth · Aurignacian
· Dimensions (body): 13.5 ×7 ×4.5 cm ·
Dimensions (head): 7 ×5 cm · Francouzská
ul., Brno II. · Moravian Museum, Brno   →

11. +12. Head of a female figure · Mammoth
· Upper Aurignacian (Gravettian) · Height:
4.8 cm · Dolní Věstonice (Mikulov District)
· Moravian Museum, Brno   ·/. →

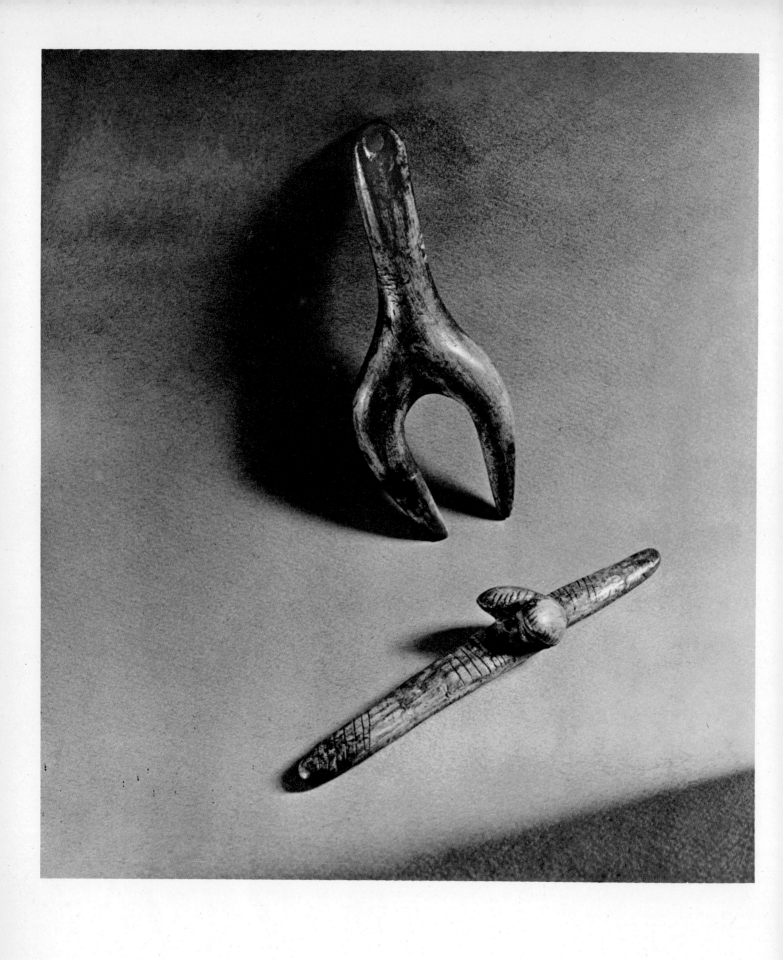

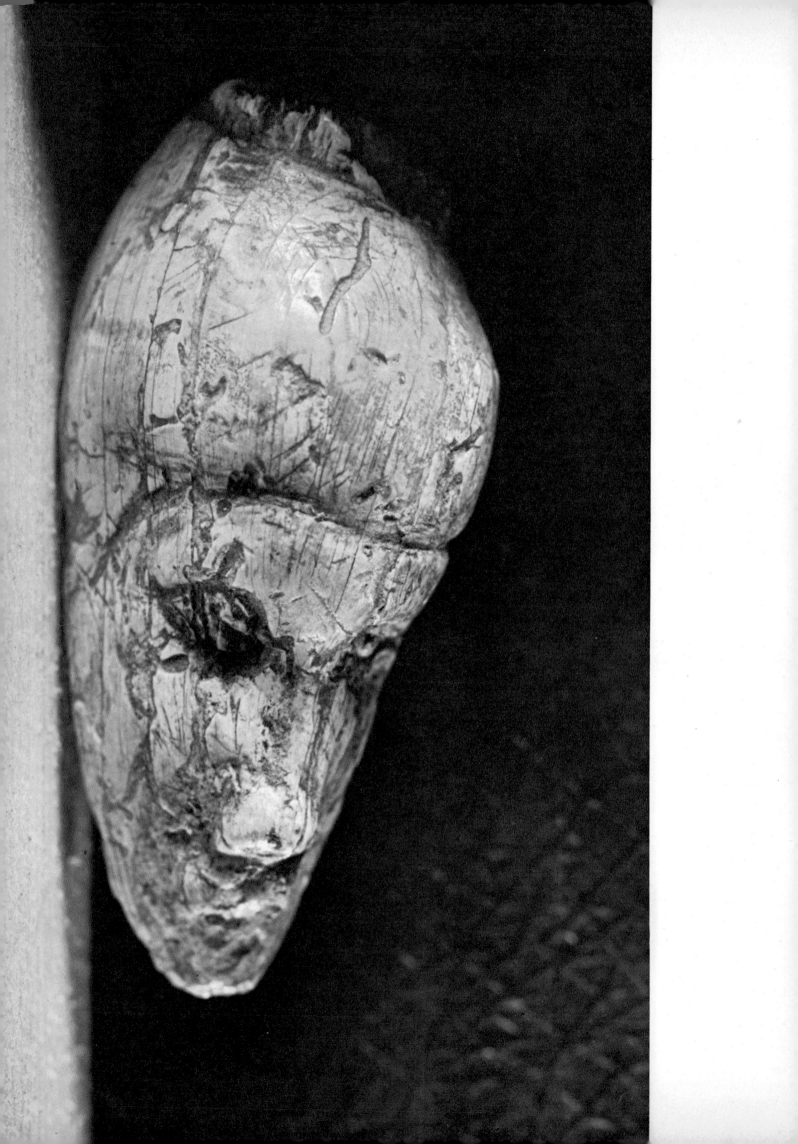

14. Lioness's head · Two deep wounds indicated · Baked clay · Upper Aurignacian (Gravettian) · Length: 4.5 cm · Dolní Věstonice (Mikulov District) · Moravian Museum, Brno

13. Statuette of a bear · Baked clay · Upper Aurignacian (Gravettian) · Length: 7.5 cm · Dolní Věstonice (Mikulov District) · Moravian Museum, Brno   ←

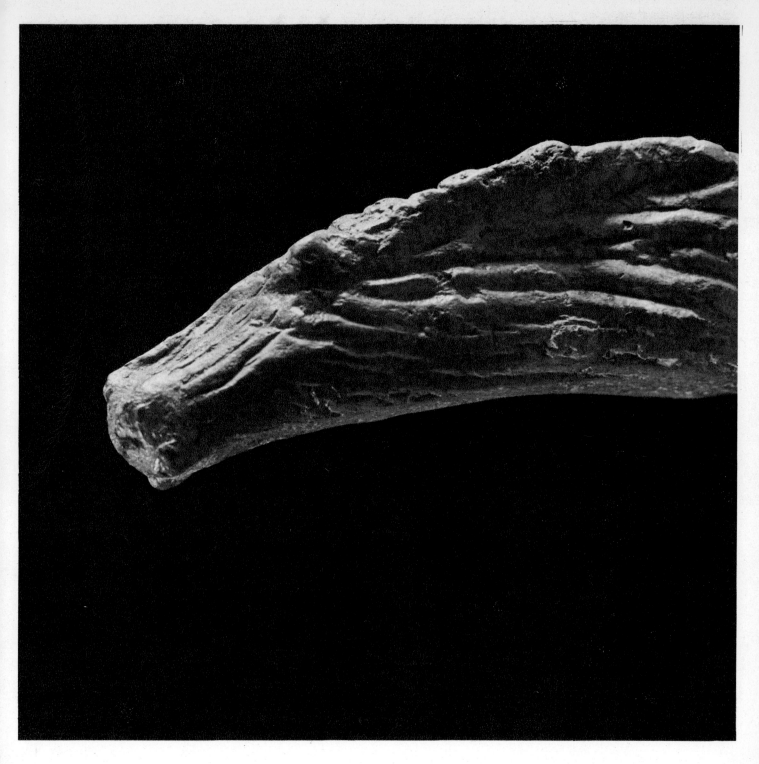

15. Horse's head and mane · Baked clay ·
Upper Aurignacian (Gravettian) · Length:
8.0 cm · Dolní Věstonice (Mikulov District)
· Moravian Museum, Brno

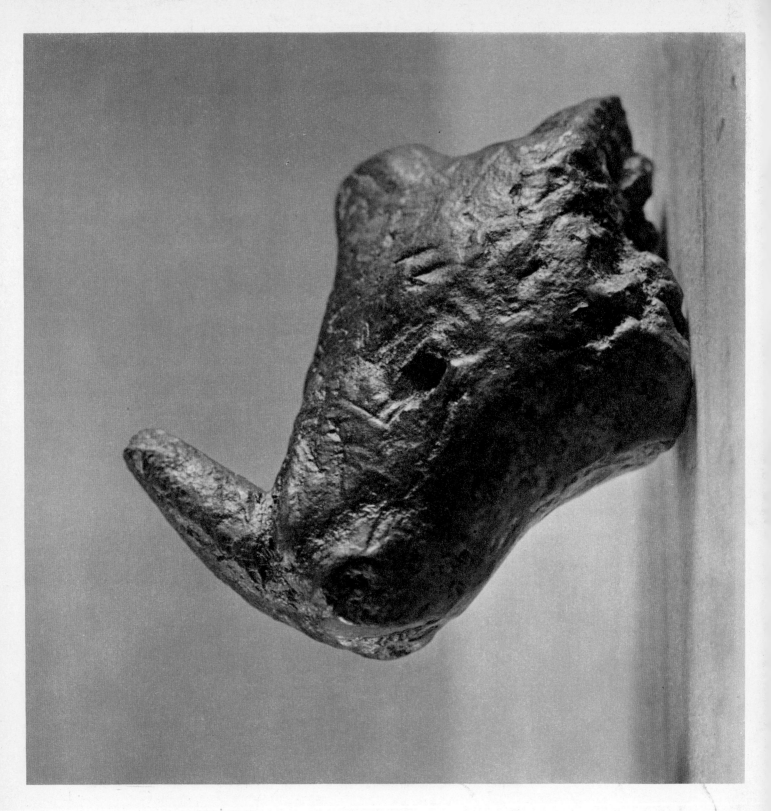

16. Rhinoceros's head · Baked clay · Upper
Aurignacian (Gravettian) · Length: 4.2 cm ·
Dolní Věstonice (Mikulov District) · Mora-
vian Museum, Brno

II. Part of neck of a vessel with well-preserved polychrome decoration · Ladle · Pottery · Neolithic. Moravian painted pottery · Height of fragment: 12.7 cm · Max. length of ladle: 15.3 cm · Střelice (Znojmo District) · Ctidružice (Moravské Budějovice District) · Moravian Museum, Brno

17. Model of a bear's head · Baked clay ·
Upper Aurignacian (Gravettian) · Length:
4.7 cm · Dolní Věstonice (Mikulov District)
· Moravian Museum, Brno

18. Extended head of a reindeer · Antlers
broken off · Baked clay · Upper Aurignacian
(Gravettian) · Length: 3.8 cm · Dolní Věstonice (Mikulov District) · Moravian Museum,
Brno   →

19. Drawing of an antelope's head · On the
same level, but at an angle of 180°, is a bison's
head · Carved on a dagger made from
a horse's jaw · Magdalenian · Dimensions of
dagger: 35 ×7.5 cm · 'Pekárna' Cave (Mokrá,
Brno District) · Moravian Museum, Brno
→

20. Drawing of a horse · Carved on a dagger
made from a horse's jawbone · Magdalenian
· Dimensions of dagger: 29 ×5.5 cm ·
'Pekárna' Cave (Mokrá, Brno District) ·
Moravian Museum, Brno   ·/. →

NEOLITHIC OR NEW STONE AGE

21. Large globular vessel · Pottery · Neolithic 'spiral' culture · Height: 28.5 cm ·
Pavlice (Znojmo District) · Moravian Museum, Brno

22. Globular vessel with four zoomorphic
lugs · Pottery · Neolithic 'spiral' culture ·
Height: 16.0 cm · Dukovany (Hrotovice
District) · Moravian Museum, Brno

III. Richly decorated beaker · Pottery ·
Chalcolithic — Bell Beaker Culture · Height:
19.7 cm · Ledce (Židlochovice District) ·
Cz. Acad. of Sciences · Arch. Inst., Brno →

23. Dish · Pottery · Neolithic 'spiral' culture
· Height: 7.5 cm · Hrotovice · Moravian
Museum, Brno

24. Gourd-shaped vessel · Pottery · Neo-
lithic 'spiral' culture · Height: 10.8 cm ·
Boskovštejn (Moravské Budějovice District)
· Moravian Museum, Brno

25. Bottle · Pottery · Neolithic 'spiral' culture · Height: 23.8 cm · Boskovštejn (Moravské Budějovice District) · Moravian Museum, Brno

26. Human figure incised on a pot · Neolithic 'spiral' culture · Height (vessel): 48.0 cm · Height (figure): 21.5 cm · Nová Ves (near Kolín) · The Dvořák Museum, Kolín →

27. Figurine — function and purpose un-
known. (Handle of a vessel?) · Baked clay ·
Neolithic 'spiral' culture · Height: 6.5 cm ·
Boskovštejn (Moravské Budějovice District)
· F. Vildomec Collection, Boskovštejn

28. Globular vessel · Pottery · Neolithic
'Bükk' culture · Height: 10.0 cm · 'Domica'
Cave (Kečovo, Šafárikovo District) · Slovak
Museum, Bratislava

29. Globular vessels · Pottery · Neolithic
'Bükk' culture · Height: 8.8 cm; 6.3 cm ·
'Domica' Cave (Kečovo, Šafárikovo Dis-
trict) · Slovak Museum, Bratislava   →

30. Pear-shaped vessel · Pottery · Neolithic
'stroke-ornamented' ware · Height: 11.4 cm
· Příkazy (Olomouc District) · Moravian
Museum, Brno

IV. Sword with cast bronze handle of anten-
nae type · Bronze · Early Hallstatt · Height
of handle: 6.5 cm · Lipovka (Rychnov nad
Kněžnou District) · National Museum,
Prague
Bracelet decorated with finely engraved ornament · Bronze · Middle Bronze Age — Tumulus Culture · Max. length: 6.5 cm · Cho-
douň u Hořovic · National Museum, Prague
·/. →

31. Pear-shaped vessel with three high-
placed handles · Pottery · Neolithic 'stroke-
ornamented' ware · Height: 14.0 cm ·
The Dvořák Museum, Kolín

32. Bucket-shaped vessel · Pottery · Neolithic 'stroke-ornamented' ware · Height:
24.7 cm · Praha-Bubeneč · Prague Muni-
cipal Museum

33. Moulded bull's head · Baked clay · Neolithic 'stroke-ornamented' ware · Height of head (snout-temple) 5.4 cm · Statenice-Černý Vůl (Prague District) · National Museum, Prague · Plaster cast. Original destroyed during the War.

34. Vessel on a hollow pedestal · Pottery ·
Neolithic Moravian painted ware · Height:
25.0 cm · Ctidružice (Moravské Budějovice
District) · Moravian Museum, Brno

35. Bowl on a low foot · Pottery with traces
of original colours on the surface · Neolithic
Moravian painted ware · Height: 12.2 cm ·
Hluboké Mašůvky (Znojmo District) · F.
Vildomec Collection, Boskovštejn

36. Tripartite vessel on a human foot ·
Pottery · Neolithic Moravian painted ware ·
Height: 15.0 cm · Hluboké Mašůvky (Znoj-
mo District) · F. Vildomec Collection,
Boskovštejn

37. Vessel with vertically perforated lug-
handles · Pottery · Neolithic Moravian
painted ware · Height: 41.5 cm · Střelice
(Znojmo District) · Moravian Museum, Brno

→

39. Hooked ladle · Pottery · Neolithic Moravian painted ware · Maximum height: 22.5 cm · Hluboké Mašůvky (Znojmo District) · F. Vildomec Collection, Boskovštejn
→

38. Vessel with well-preserved coloured decoration · Pottery · Neolithic Moravian painted ware · Height: 10.8 cm · Střelice (Znojmo District) · F. Vildomec Collection, Boskovštejn

42. Amphora · Pottery · Neolithic 'Theiss'
Culture · Height: 16.2 cm · Slatinka nad
Bebravou, Slovakia ·Slovak Museum, Martin

43. Vessel with tall shoulder, decorated with
three knobs on widest part · Pottery · Neolithic Moravian painted ware · Height:
29.5 cm · Hluboké Mašůvky (Znojmo District) · F. Vildomec, Boskovštejn →

40. Vase with zoomorphic lugs and human
figures in 'pricked' technique · Pottery ·
Neolithic Moravian painted ware · Height:
38.0 cm · Střelice (Znojmo District) · F. Vildomec Collection, Boskovštejn   ←

41. Square vessel with feet · Pottery · Neolithic Moravian painted ware · Height:
17.2 cm · Provenance unknown · Moravian
Museum, Brno

V. Heavy compound spiral brooch · Bronze
· Late Bronze Age · Lusatian Culture · Max.
length: 23.6 cm · Jaroměř, Bohemia ·
National Museum, Prague   ·/. ←

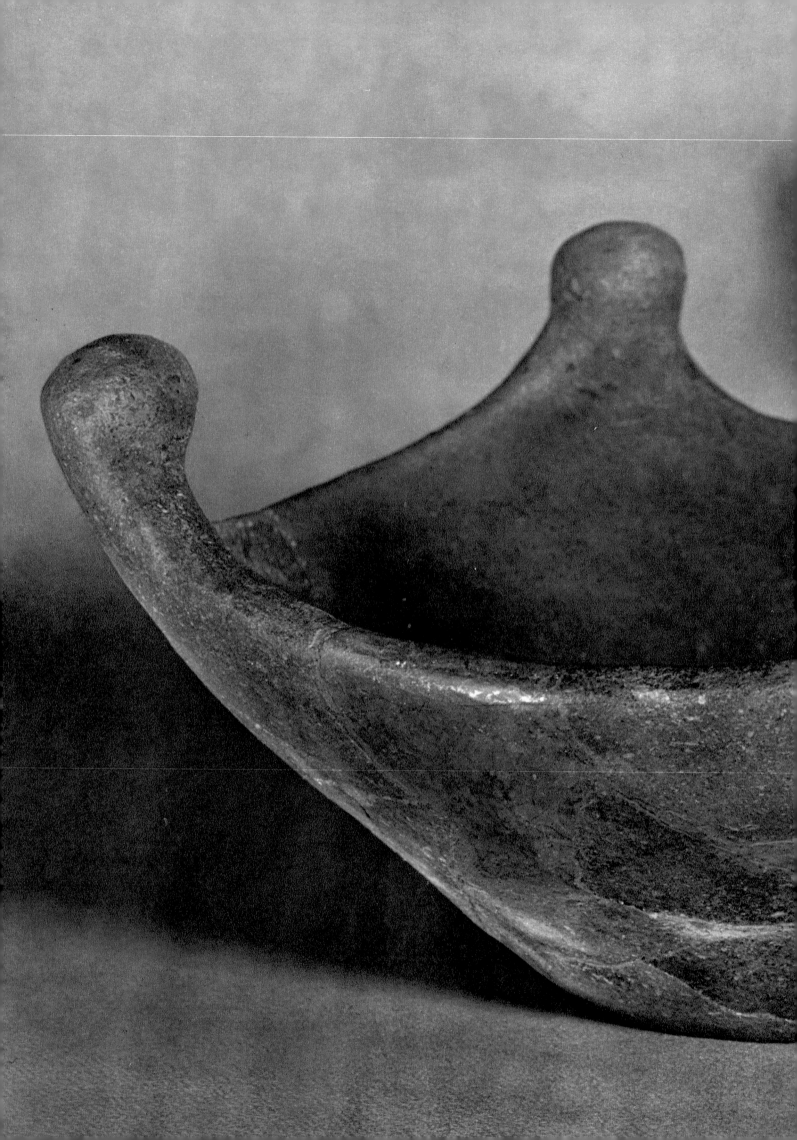

45. Cubical object with a round hollow in the middle · Lamp? · Baked clay · Neolithic Moravian painted ware · Height: 6.8 cm · Jaroměřice nad Rokytnou (Moravské Budějovice District) · Moravian Museum, Brno

46. Female figurines showing extreme stylization and exaggeration of the lower parts · Baked clay · Neolithic Moravian painted ware · Height: 21.0 cm; 22.0 cm · Střelice (Znojmo District) · Moravian Museum, Brno
→

44. Bowl with four decorative horns · Pottery · Neolithic Moravian painted ware · Maximum height: 13.0 cm · Hluboké Mašůvky (Znojmo District) · F. Vildomec Collection, Boskovštejn
← ·/.

48. Torso of stylised female figure · Baked clay · Neolithic Moravian painted ware · Height: 7.3 cm · Střelice (Znojmo District) · Moravian Museum, Brno

47. Stylised female figure · Baked clay · Neolithic Moravian painted ware · Height: 15.5 cm · Střelice (Znojmo District) · Moravian Museum, Brno ←

49. +50. Human figure with stylised hair-
dress · Baked clay · Lengyel culture ·
Piešťany Museum, Slovakia

VI. Various vessels · Pottery · Late Hallstatt · Bylany Culture · Hradeníny (Kolín
District) · Dvořák Museum, Kolín   ·/. →

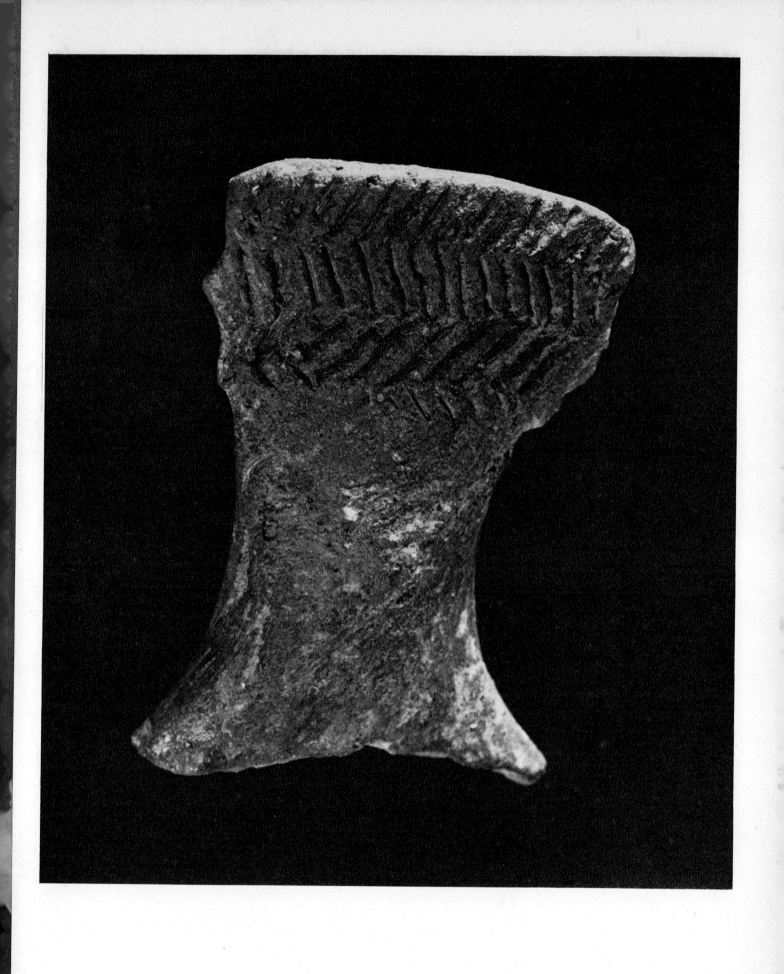

51. Female statuette. (In posture of adoration?) · Baked clay · Neolithic Moravian painted ware · Height: 36.0 cm · F. Vildomec Collection, Hluboké Mašůvky

52. Detail of the statuette from pl. 51

54. Small model of a human head · Baked
clay · Neolithic Moravian painted ware ·
Height: 6 cm · F. Vildomec Collection

53. Expressive stylised female figure with
holes in the eyesockets · Baked clay · Neolithic Moravian painted ware · Height:
8.8 cm · Štěpánovice (Moravské Budějovice
District) · Moravian Museum, Brno   ←

55. Small heads modelled in clay · Baked clay
· Neolithic Moravian painted ware · Heights:
6.5; 5.5; 6.5; 7.5 cm · Jaroměřice nad Rokytnou · Moravian Museum, Brno   ·/. →

56. + 57. Figurine with flat back containing
a round opening · Baked clay · Neolithic
Moravian painted ware · Maximum height:
12.7 cm · Kroměříž · Moravian Museum,
Brno

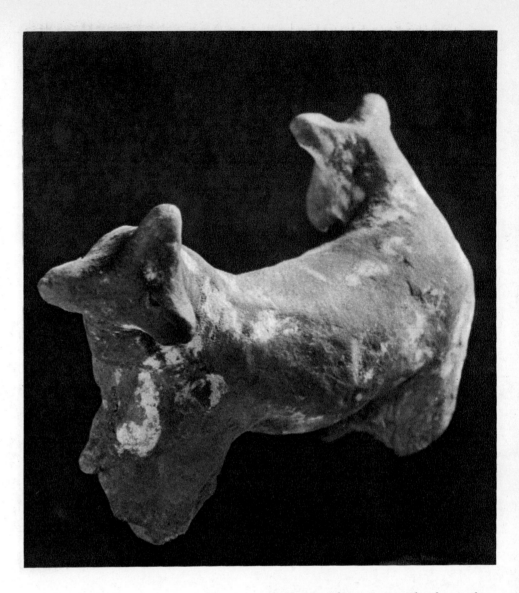

59. Handle of a vessel in the form of an animal · Baked clay · Neolithic Moravian painted ware · Height of face: 3.2 cm · Kramolín (Náměšť nad Oslavou District) · Museum in Třebíč

58. Zoomorphic vessel representing a boar (bear?) · Baked clay · Lengyel culture · Height: 20.4 cm; length: 20.0 cm; breadth: 16.3 cm · Abraham (Slovakia) · Piešťany Museum   ←

VII. Stylised animal figure on an object of unidentified purpose · Bronze · Late Hallstatt · Platěnice Culture · Length of figurine: c. 4.5 cm · Hradenín (Kolín District) · The Dvořák Museum, Kolín   ·/. ←

60. Broken-off lug of a lid · Pottery · Neolithic Moravian painted ware · Length:
5.5 cm · Kostelec by Prostějov · Museum
in Olomouc

61. Prehistoric model of a hut with gabled
roof · Pottery · Neolithic Moravian painted
ware · Height: 12.0 cm; breadth: 11.0 cm;
length: 15.0 cm · Střelice (Znojmo District) ·
Moravian Museum, Brno   →

CHALCOLITHIC OR LATE STONE AGE

62. Jug with tall neck and shallow, flattened
body · Pottery · Chalcolithic 'Channelled
Ware' · Height: 16.0 cm · Prague-Vinohrady
· National Museum, Prague

63. Vase · Pottery · Chalcolithic 'Channelled Ware' · Height: 37.3 cm · Topolčany (Slovakia) · Slovak Museum, Martin ←

64. Small jug with a broad handle · Pottery · Chalcolithic 'Channelled Ware' · Height: 13 cm · Moravské Lieskové, Slovakia · Slovak Museum, Martin

66. Gourd-shaped dish · Pottery · Traces of the original white incrustation in the grooves · Chalcolithic 'Laibacher Moor' Culture · Height: 9.1 cm · Velké Kostelany, Slovakia · Slovak Museum, Martin

VIII. Bronze chain with hook for suspension · La Tène · Holiare, Slovakia (Čalovo District) · Archæological Institute, Nitra →

65. Cylindrical vessel with everted rim · Vessel with four horns at widest part · Amphora · Jug with broad handle · Pottery · Chalcolithic 'Michelsberg' culture · Height: 9.0; 8.7; 10.5; 25.0 cm · Jug: Hradenín. Other objects: Bylany-Okrouhlík (near Kolín) · The Dvořák Museum, Kolín ←

68. Vessel with a strongly-marked bulge decorated with plastic ribs · Pottery · Chalcolithic · Height: 19.5 cm · Prostějov · Museum in Olomouc →

67. Dish on a foot · Baked clay · Neolithic 'Laibacher Moor' Culture · Height: 8.0 cm · Bylany-Okrouhlík (near Kolín) · The Dvořák Museum, Kolín

69. Low jug decorated on the body with
plastic ribs · Pottery · Chalcolithic 'Channelled Ware' · Height: 15 cm · Charváty
(Olomouc District) · Museum in Olomouc

70. Jug with handle of the 'ansa lunata' type
· Pottery · Chalcolithic · Height: 19.5 cm ·
Ďáblice (Prague District) · National Mu-
seum, Prague   →

71. Vessel with finely smoothed surface ·
Pottery · Chalcolithic 'Jevišovice' Culture ·
Height: 18.4 cm · Jevišovice (Znojmo Dis-
trict) · Moravian Museum, Brno

72. Stylised animal head · Handle of a vessel?
(figurine?) · Baked clay · Chalcolithic 'Jevišovice' culture · Height of face: 7.5 cm ·
Jevišovice (Moravské Budějovice District) ·
Moravian Museum, Brno   →

73. Upper part of amphora - richly decorated · Pottery · Chalcolithic 'globular
amphora' culture · Height of part illustrat-
ed: 13.3 cm · Vicinity of Kolín · The
Dvořák Museum, Kolín   →

IX. Large perforated bead with knob-like excrescences · Vitreous substance · La Tène · Height: 4.0 cm · Vícenice, near Klatovy · National Museum, Prague

74. Thin-walled vessel decorated with cord impressions · Pottery · Chalcolithic corded ware · Height: 13.2 cm · Nemotice (Bučovice District) · Moravian Museum, Brno ←

75. Jug with broad handle, with incised decoration · Pottery · Chalcolithic corded ware · Height: 25.8 cm · Sivice (Brno District) · Moravian Museum, Brno

76. Jug · Pottery · Chalcolithic 'Bell Beaker'
culture · Height: 12.4 cm · Šlapanice (Brno
District) · Moravian Museum, Brno

EARLY TO LATE BRONZE AGE

77. Cup decorated with fine slip · Pottery ·
Early Bronze Age 'Únětice' culture · Height:
6.0 cm · Lednice (Mikulov District) · Moravian Museum, Brno

78. Cups with widely everted rim and
flattened bodies · Pottery · Early Bronze
Age 'Maďarovce' culture · Height: 6.2 cm ·
Veselé (Piešťany District)

79. Vase with everted rim · Pottery · Early
Bronze Age 'Maďarovce' culture · Height:
14.0 cm · Nitranský Hrádok, Slovakia

80. Waisted jug with everted rim · Pottery ·
Early-Middle Bronze Age 'North Panno-
nian' culture · Height: 14.0 cm · Nitranský
Hrádok, Slovakia · Slovak Academy of
Sciences, Archaeological Institute, Nitra ·
Two-handled vessel with perforated base ·
Pottery · Early Bronze Age 'Maďarovce'
culture · Height: 5.5 cm · Nitranský Hrá-
dok, Slovakia · Slovak Academy of Sciences,
Archaeological Institute, Nitra   ·/. →

X. Glass goblet · Roman Period, 1st cent. —
Height: 18 cm · Vysoká pri Morave · Slovak
Museum, Bratislava   →

80a. Vessel with incised and white incrusted
ornament · Middle Bronze Age · Height:
21.5 cm · Vacíkov (Blatná District) · National Museum, Prague

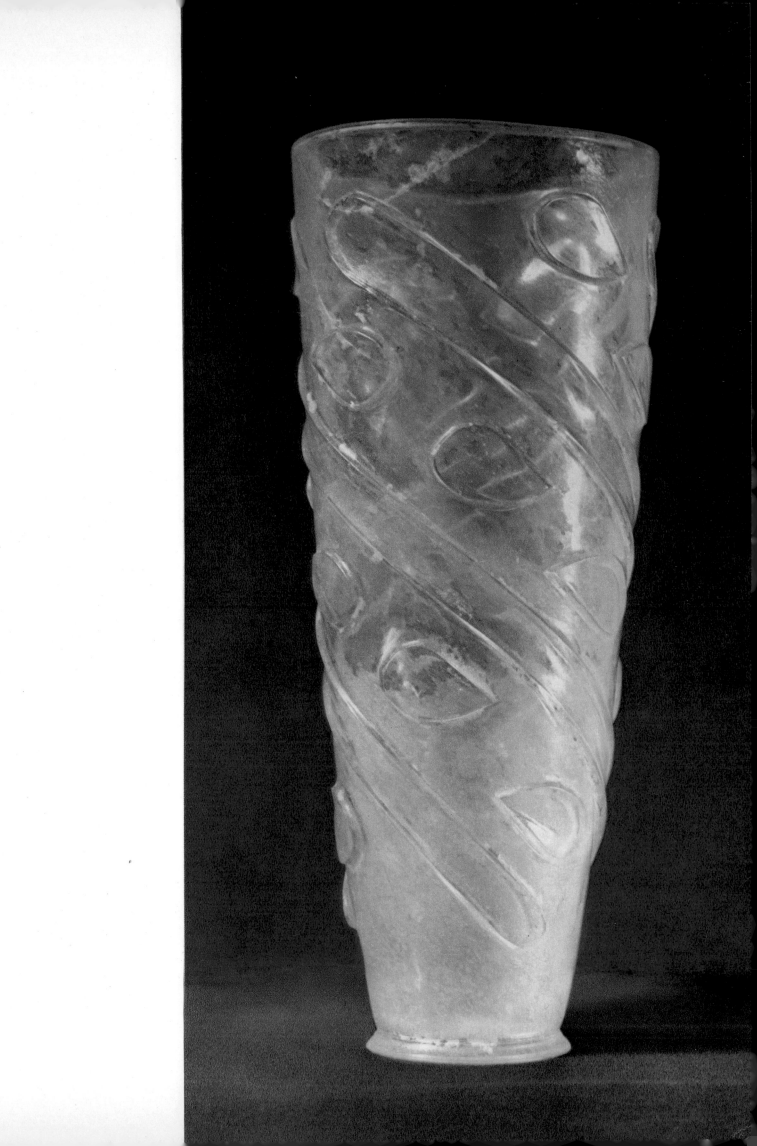

81. Bone ring decorated with bands of wavy ornament in relief · Early Bronze Age 'Věteřov' culture · Height: 5.0 cm · Blučina (Židlochovice District) · Moravian Museum, Brno ←

82. Two-handled vessel with vertical ribs on the body · Pottery · Middle Bronze Age 'Tumulus' Culture · Height: about 27 cm · Hrušky (Břeclav District) · Moravian Museum Brno

83. Jug with everted rim · Pottery · Middle Bronze Age 'Tumulus' culture · Height: 13.0 cm · Jiříkovice by Brno · Moravian Museum, Brno

84. Small jug with everted rim, curved neck and well-preserved white incrustation · Pottery · Early-Middle Bronze Age 'Kisapostag' culture · Height: 10.0 cm · Hurbanovo, Slovakia · Slovak Academy of Sciences, Archaeological Institute, Nitra →

85. Vase with one small perforated lug · Pottery · Early-Middle Bronze Age 'North Pannonian' culture · Height: 9.0 cm · Velký Harčáš, Slovakia · Slovak Museum, Bratislava

86. Jug with everted rim · Pottery · Early-Middle Bronze Age 'North Pannonian' culture · Height: 14.7 cm · Velký Harčáš, Slovakia · Slovak Museum, Martin →

87. Biconical vessel with rough channelling
on the lower part · Pottery · Late Bronze
'Lusatian' culture · Height: 28.5 cm · Švá-
benice (Vyškov District) · Czechoslovak
Academy of Sciences, Arch. Inst., Brno

88. Two-handled amphora with two perforated lugs and vertical ribs in relief · Pottery · Early Bronze Age (Lusatian culture) · Height: 31.0 cm · Moravičany (Zábřeh District) · Czechosl. Acad. of Sciences, Arch. Inst., Brno

89. Bottom of a vessel with rich moulded,
grooved and incised decoration · Pottery ·
Early-Middle Bronze Age 'Upper Theiss'
culture · Diameter: 27.7 cm · Bracovce, Slovakia · Slovak Museum, Martin

XI. Goblet with everted rim · Glass · Migration Period · 5th cent. A. D. · Height:
9.0 cm · Brno-Černá Pole · Moravian
Museum, Brno   →

90. Zoomorphic vessel · Pottery · Late
Bronze Age · Height: 12.0 cm · Hrubčice
(Prostějov District) · Museum in Olomouc

91. Biconical vessel with lid · In the vessel
and lid there are corresponding openings ·
Pottery · Late Bronze Age · Height: 95 cm ·
Bylany-Okrouhlík (Kolín District) · The
Dvořák Museum, Kolín   →

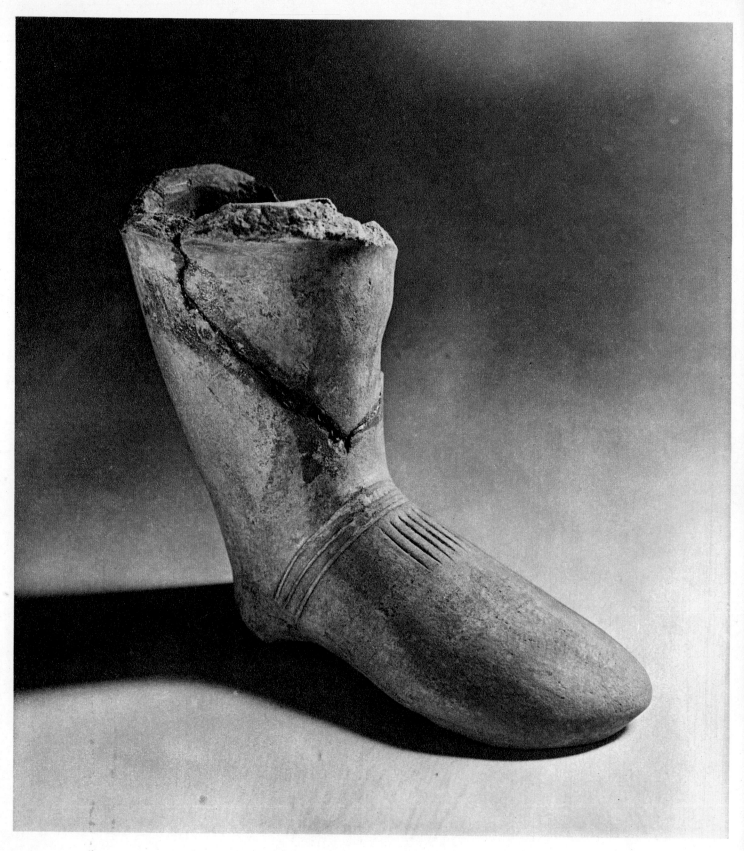

92. Model of a booted human foot · (Foot of a vessel?) · Baked clay · Early Bronze Age · 'Lusatian' culture · Height: 8.5 cm · Násedlovice u Kyjova · Moravian Museum, Brno

93. Cast sword hilt with relief and incised decoration · Bronze · Late Bronze Age · Height of the hilt: 10.5 cm · Vyšný Sliač (Ružomberok District) · Slovak Acad. of Sciences, Arch. Inst., Nitra　→

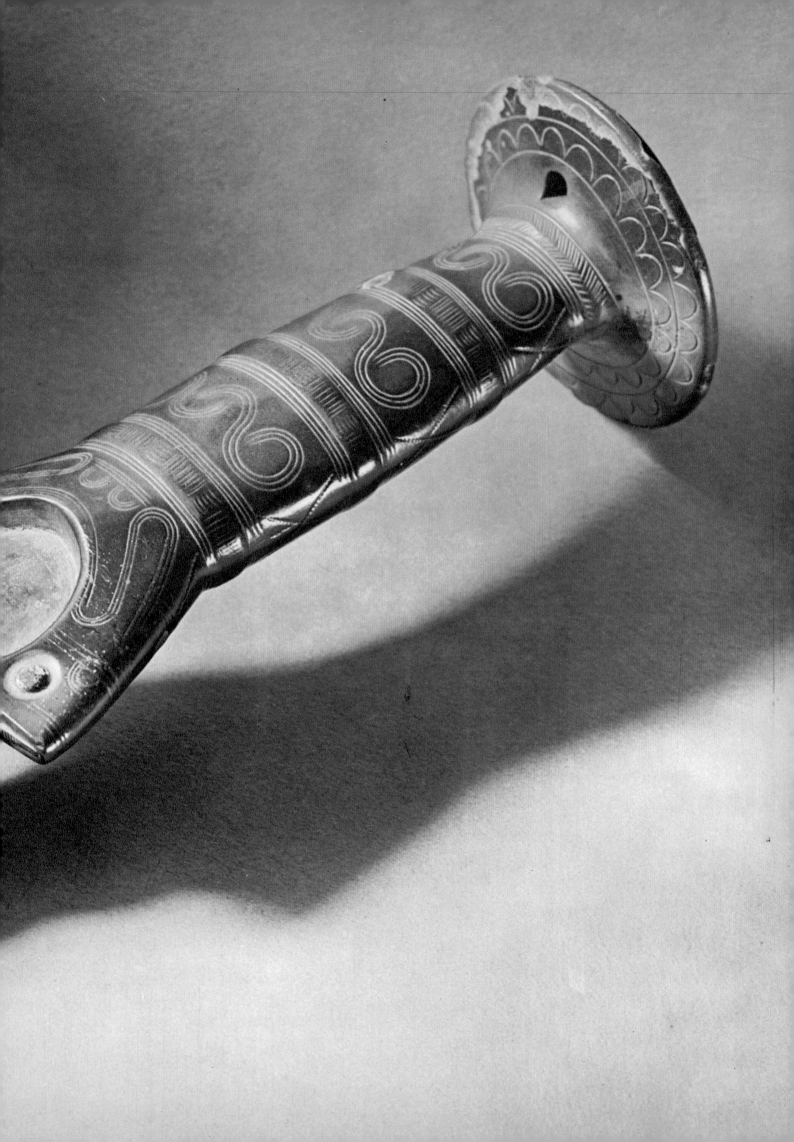

95. Massive bronze bracelet with straight ends, the coils being reinforced with a moulded mid-rib · Late Bronze Age · Height: 14.5 cm · Křenůvky (Prostějov District) · Museum in Olomouc

94. Sword hilt, finely engraved · Bronze · Late Bronze Age · Height of hilt: 10.8 cm · Komjatná (Ružomberok District) · Slovak Museum, Martin · ˙/. ←

96. Massive bracelet · Bronze · Late Bronze
Age · Maximum height: 13.0 cm · Přestavlky
(Přerov District) · Moravian Museum, Brno

97. Massive spiral ornament · Bronze · Late
Bronze Age · Diameter: 13.7 cm · Krasná
Horka-Nedvedzie, Slovakia · Slovak Mu-
seum, Martin

XII. Goblet of tall, slim type · Glass · Migration Period · 5th—6th cent. A. D. · Height:
27.5 cm · Prague, Kobylisy · National Museum, Prague ·/. →

98. Massive personal ornament. (Diadem? Collar?) · Bronze · Late Bronze Age (Early Hallstatt) · Diameter: 16.5 cm · Sliač (Ružomberok District)·Slovak Museum, Martin

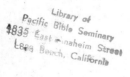

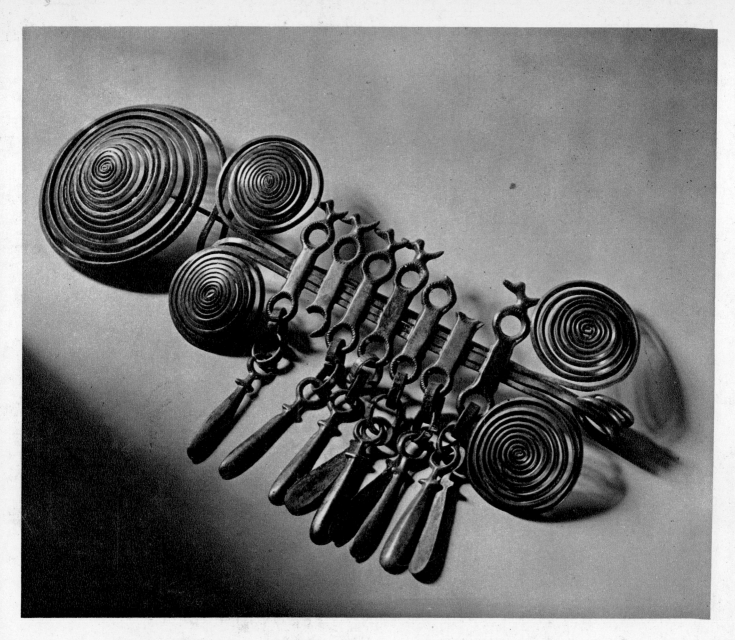

99. Splendid spiral brooch · Bronze · Late
Bronze Age (Early Hallstatt) · Length:
37.0 cm · Krivoklat (Púchov District) ·
Slovak Museum, Martin

100. Tall conical helmet · Beaten bronze,
2 mm thick · Early Hallstatt · Height:
21.5 cm · Slovak Museum, Martin · Site
unknown   →

101. Rectangular plaque decorated with fine
engraving. (Belt ornament?) · Bronze · Late
Bronze Age · Dimensions: 15.1 ×7.3 cm ·
Přestavlky (Přerov District) · Moravian Museum, Brno
Disk-headed pin with incised spiral decoration · Bronze · Middle Bronze Age · Length:
18.3 cm · Hradisko by Kroměříž · Moravian
Museum, Brno   ·/. →

HALLSTATT—EARLY IRON AGE

102. Cup with ribbon handle · Pottery · Late
Bronze Age — Early Hallstatt 'Velatice'
culture · Height: 4.5 cm · Velatice (Brno
District) · Moravian Museum, Brno

103. Small vessel on human feet with high-set handles · Pottery · Late Bronze Age — Early Hallstatt 'Velatice' culture · Height (base to rim): 8.1 cm · Lednice (Mikulov District) · Moravian Museum, Brno ←

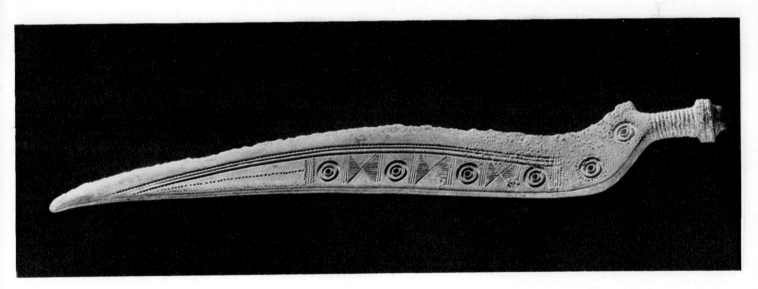

104. Knife with curved back and engraved design · Bronze · Early Hallstatt · Length: 20.0 cm · Klentnice (Mikulov District) · Cz. Acad. of Sciences, Arch. Inst., Brno

105. Zoomorphic vessel ornamented with
pricked and grooved design · Pottery ·
Early Hallstatt · Height: 13.6 cm · Kolínsko
(Details unknown) · The Dvořák Museum,
Kolín

XIII. Coloured necklace · Glass, amber,
semi-precious stones · Migration Period ·
5th cent. A. D. · Diameter of largest bead:
3.5 cm · Znojmo · Moravian Museum, Brno

107. Cup decorated on the outside with tin open-work · Bronze · Early Hallstatt · Height: 5.1 cm · Náklo (Litovel District) · Museum in Olomouc

106. Amphora with polished graphite surface · Pottery · Early Hallstatt · Height: 12.5 cm · Brno-Obřany · Moravian Museum, Brno   ←

108. Bracelet ending in a double pair of em-
bossed (repoussé) spirals · Bronze · Early
Hallstatt · Diameter: 23.0 cm · Turčianská
Blatnica (Martin District) · Slovak Museum,
Martin

109. Front of a massive brooch · Bronze ·
Early Hallstatt · Length: 32.8 cm · Krásná
Horka (Trstená District) · Slovak Museum,
Martin

110. Double vessel with single handle ·
Pottery · Hallstatt · 'Podolí' culture ·
Height: 10.0 cm · Brno-Obřany · Moravian
Museum, Brno

111. Double vessel joined at the body and
with a horizontal handle · Pottery · Hallstatt · 'Podolí' culture · Height: 9.4 cm ·
Mužla (Štúrovo District) · Sl. Acad. of
Sciences — Arch. Inst., Nitra

113. Zoomorphic vessel with slightly deformed body · Pottery · Hallstatt · Height:
15.5 cm · Chotín, Slovakia · S. A. S. —
A. I., Nitra

112. Fragment of a zoomorphic cult object
from a hearth (?) · Baked clay · Hallstatt ·
Maximum height: 17.7 cm · Brno Obřany ·
Moravian Museum, Brno   ←

114. Low jug with grooved decoration ·
Pottery · Hallstatt · Height: 10.0 cm ·
Bereksek (Hlohovec District) · Slovak Mu-
seum, Martin

XIV. Several objects from a rich, intact
grave · Gold, almandines, silver · Migration
Period · 5th cent. A. D. · Length of the end
of belt: 17.0 cm · Blučina (Židlochovice) ·
Moravian Museum, Brno   →

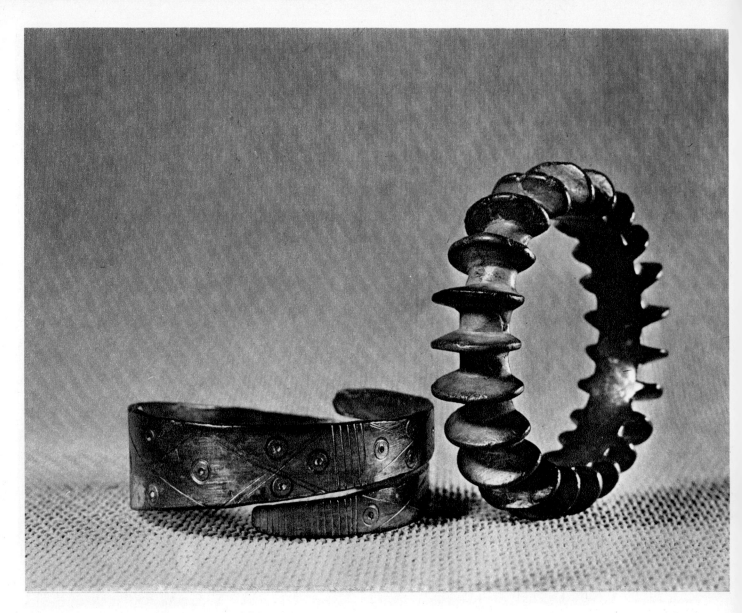

115. Bracelet of bronze with tapering ends.
Engraved design on outer side · Hallstatt ·
Diameter: 7.8 cm · Hostýn (Near Bystřice
pod Hostýnem) · Moravian Museum,
Brno
Massive lobed bracelet · Bronze · Late Hall-
statt · Diameter: 8.4 cm · Býčí skála near
Adamov · Moravian Museum, Brno

116. Bone object, function and purpose unknown, engraved with scene of a chariot
drawn by a pair of horses · Late Hallstatt ·
Length: 16.5 cm · Dobrčice by Přerov ·
Moravian Museum, Brno   →

117. Stylised figure of a horse · Bronze ·
Hallstatt · 'Podolí' culture · Maximum
height: 9.0 cm · Brno-Obřany · Moravian
Museum, Brno   ·/. →

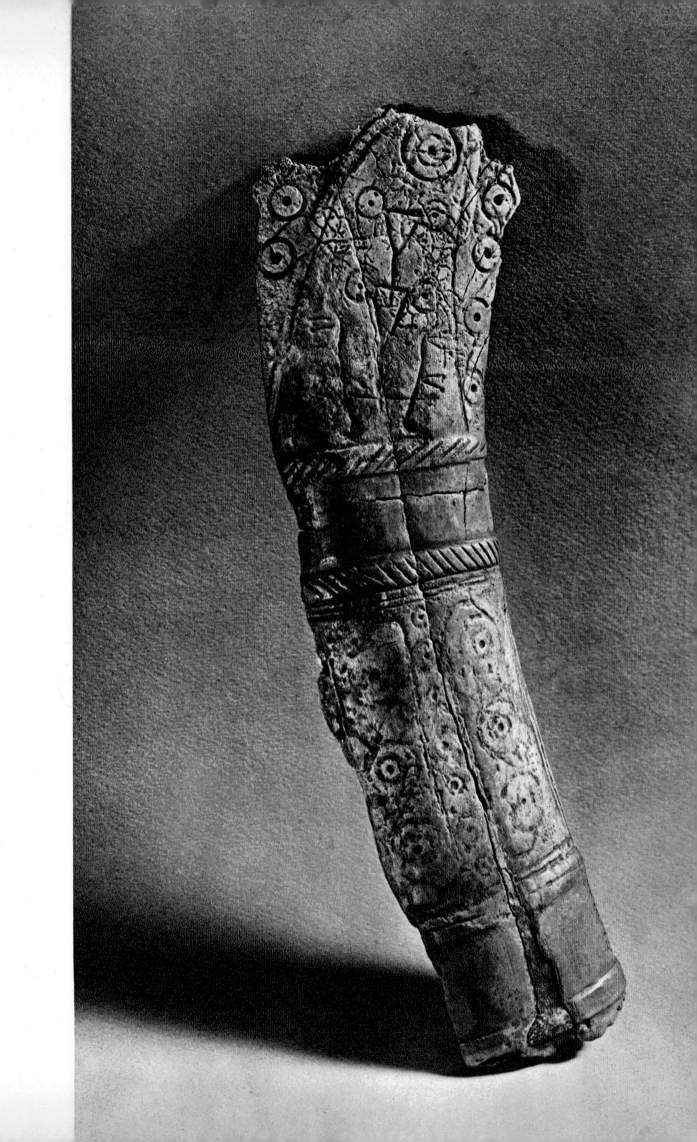

118. Cast of a small bull figurine · Original material: bronze · Late Hallstatt · Height: 7.5 cm · Býčí skála near Adamov · Original in the Natural History Museum, Vienna

119. Rim of plate decorated with stylised swans and sun symbols · Bronze · Late Hallstatt Period · 'Horákov' culture · Rim: 8 cm · Horákov near Brno · Moravian Museum, Brno   ·/. →

120. Stylised swan with two pendants below the beak · Bronze · Late Hallstatt · 'Platěnice' culture · Height: 9.0 cm · Svijany by Turnov · National Museum, Prague

XV. Dagger sheath, end of belt and ring · Decorated with gold and coloured enamels · Slavonic culture ı· 2nd half of 9th cent. · Length of sheath: 13.2 cm · Staré Město-Uherské Hradiště · Moravian Museum, Brno

·/· →

122. Pendant in the form of an animal ·
Bronze · Late Hallstatt · 'Platěnice' Culture
· Length: 3.5 cm · Mohelnice (District Zá-
břeh) · Cz. Acad. of Sciences — Arch. Inst.,
Brno

121. Various vessels · Pottery · Late Hallstatt
· 'Bylany' culture · Dvořák Museum, Kolín
←

LA TÈNE CULTURE

123. Small metal plaque decorated with fine engraving and grotesque human face · Bronze · Early La Tène · Length: about 7.0 cm · Stupava, Slovakia · Slovak Museum, Bratislava

124. Zoomorphic brooch with traces of white enamel · Bronze · Early La Tène · Length: 7.0 cm · Chýnovský Háj near Libčice (Prague District) · National Museum, Prague   ←

125. Sherds decorated with fine engraved and pricked design · Hard baked clay · Early La Tène · Dimensions: 7.5 ×11.3 cm; 8.2 ×7.3 cm, 6.3 ×11.2 cm · Koryčany (Kyjov District) · Moravian Museum, Brno

126. Amphora and two jugs · Pottery · Scythian Culture · Height: 9.5 cm; 10.5 cm; 10.5 cm · Chotín (Komárno District) · Sl. Acad. of Sciences, Arch. Inst., Nitra

127. Three bracelets and two richly ornamented brooches · Bronze · La Tène ·
Dimensions: max. diameter: 8.5 cm; axis:
10.6—9.4 cm; diameter: 9.2 cm; length:
7.7 cm, length: 6.2 cm · Moravian Museum,
Brno

128. Piece of metal-work with grotesque and caricatured human face · Bronze · La Tène · Height of face: 2.5 cm · Brno-Maloměřice · Moravian Museum, Brno

129. Sculpture of a man's head · Clay stone · La Tène · Height: 23.5 cm · Mšecké Žehrovice near Slaný · National Museum, Prague →

XVI. Jewellery from Slavonic graves · Gold, silver, bronze, glass · Slavonic Culture, 2nd half of the 9th cent. · Max. diameter of silver crescent pendant: 9.1 cm · Staré Město-Uherské Hradiště · Moravian Museum, Brno · The crescent pendant is from the cemetery at Dolní Věstonice (Mikulov District) ·/. →

131. Piece of metal-work ornamented with bird's head · Bronze · La Tène · Maximum diameter: 11.8 cm · Brno-Maloměřice · Moravian Museum, Brno

130. Piece of metal-work with exaggeratedly stylised animal figure · Bronze · La Tène · Height of face: 1.8 cm · Brno-Maloměřice · Moravian Museum, Brno ←

132. Deep pedestalled dish · Pottery · La
Tène culture · Height: 21.5 cm · Vicinity
of Kolín · The Dvořák Museum, Kolín

133. Bottle with polished surface · Pottery ·
La Tène · Height: 25.0 cm · Černov near
Slaný · National Museum, Prague   →

135. Large vase with incised decoration ·
Pottery · La Tène · Height: 57.5 cm · Vy-
soká pri Morave, Slovakia · Slovak Museum,
Bratislava →

134. Broad bottle with polished surface ·
Pottery · La Tène · Height: 23.3 cm · Velká
Maňa (Zlaté Moravce District) · Slovak Mu-
seum, Bratislava

136. Statuette of a boar · Bronze · La Tène ·
Length: 11.6 cm · Prague-Šárka · National
Museum, Prague   ·/. ←

137. Stylisation of an elongated animal figure
· Bronze · Late La Tène Period · Length:
7.3 cm · Stradonice · National Museum,
Prague

138. Small figure carrying unidentified object on shoulder · Bronze · Late La Tène · Height: 4.5 cm · Stradonice · National Museum, Prague

139. Celtic coin found in Bohemia · Numis-
matic Dept. of the Nat. Museum, Prague

140. Small dog and boar designed as pendants · Bronze · Late La Tène · Length: dog 4.9 cm; boar 3.5 cm · Čejkovice (Hodonín District) · Provenance of boar unknown; Moravian Museum, Brno

CONTACT WITH THE ROMAN EMPIRE

141. (←) 142. Bronze flagon with female figu-
rine · Roman Period · First half of 1st cent. ·
Height: 14.6 cm · Praha-Bubeneč · National
Museum, Prague

143. Dish on a tall stem · Pottery · Roman
Period 1st cent. · Height: 14.0 cm · Plaňany
by Kolín · The Dvořák Museum, Kolín

144. Tile with stamp of the XVth Legion ·
Baked clay · Roman Period. 2nd cent. ·
Length of upper edge of stamp: 9.5 cm ·
Stupava, Slovakia · Slovak Museum, Brati-
slava

145. Sherd with incised figure of a running
animal · Baked clay · Roman Period. 2nd
cent. · Height of sherd: 13.0 cm ·Příkazy
(Olomouc District) · Moravian Museum
Brno   →

147. Dish with raised moulded knobs and rough plaiting · Pottery · Roman Period · 3rd cent. · Height: 19.5 cm · Šaratice (Slavkov District) · Moravian Museum, Brno ←

148. Bowl · Fine loess · Roman Period. 3rd cent. · Height: 17.5 cm · Kostelec na Hané · Museum in Olomouc

149. Brooches richly decorated with granulation · Gold · Roman Period · First half of 4th cent. · Length: 5 cm · Stráže (Grave I), Slovakia · Museum in Piešťany

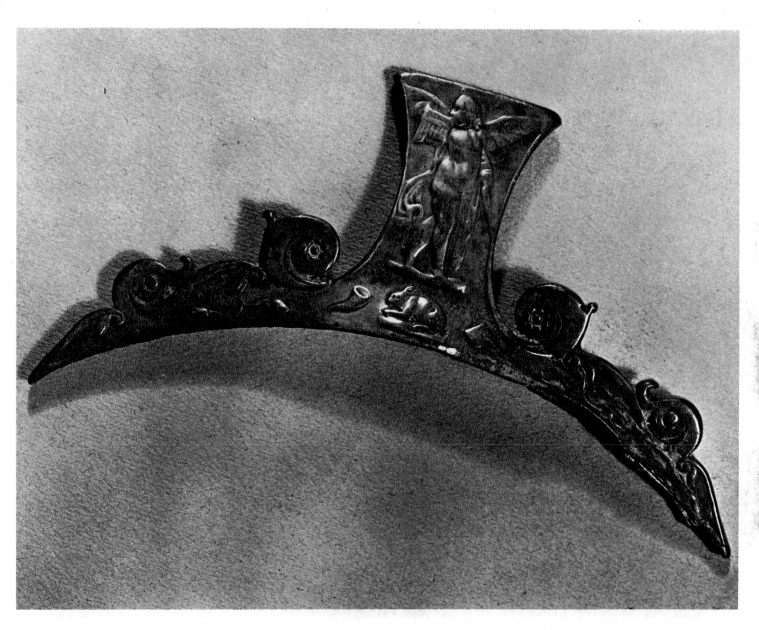

150. Upper metal-work ornament on a glass goblet (Kantharos) · Silver · Roman Period. 4th cent. · Stráže (Grave II), Slovakia · Museum in Piešťany

151. Glass dish · Roman Period · First
half of 4th cent. · Stráže (Grave I),
Slovakia · Museum in Piešťany

PERIOD OF THE 'MIGRATION OF PEOPLES'

153. Bowl with incised ornament · Pottery ·
4th cent. · Height: 17.7 cm · Brno-Obřany ·
Moravian Museum, Brno

152. Jar with broad, flat rim · Pottery · 4th
cent. · Height: 43.5 cm · Brno-Obřany ·
Moravian Museum, Brno   ·/. ←

XIX. Circular medallion with figure scene in repoussé work · Silver · Slavonic Culture · 2nd half of 9th cent. · Diameter 4.3 cm · Staré Město—Uherské Hradiště, from 'Na Špitalkách' Church · Moravian Museum, Brno

154. Clasp with notched decoration · Gilded
bronze · 5th cent. · Length: 13.8 cm · Museum
in Košice

155. Jug · Well-baked loess · 5th cent. ·
Height: 19.0 cm · Museum in Košice ·
Details of site unknown   →

156. Fragment of ornament with plaited
design · Wood · 5th—6th cent. · Length:
12.5 cm · Žuráň (Podolí, near Brno) · Moravian Museum, Brno

157—159. Fragments of a pyxis decorated
with figures · Ivory · 5th—6th cent. · Height:
10.0 cm · Žuráň (Podolí, near Brno) · Cz.
Acad. of Sciences—Arch. Inst., Brno   →

157—159. Fragments of a pyxis decorated with figures · Ivory · 5th—6th cent. · Height: 10.0 cm · Žuráň (Podolí, near Brno) · Cz. Acad. of Sciences—Arch. Inst., Brno

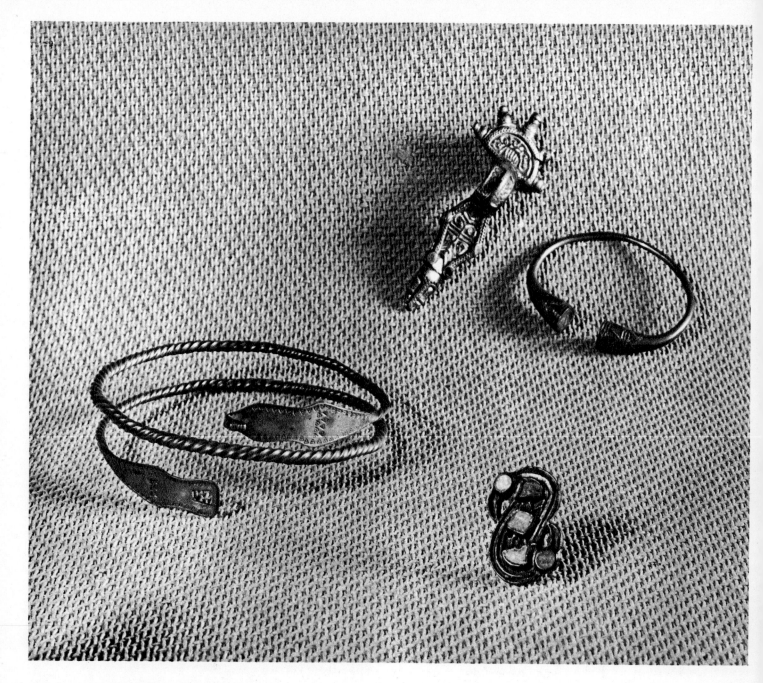

160. Jewellery from Migration Period. 6th cent. · Silver elliptical bangle with seal terminations · Axis: 6.4 × 5.4 cm · Silver bracelet of stout twisted wire with embossed ends · Diameter: 9.7 cm · Both objects: Poštorná (Břeclav District) · Silver clasp, decorated with notching · Stylised human head at the bottom · Silver of inferior quality · Length: 9.6 cm · Šlapanice (Brno) · S-shaped clasp, decorated with notching, gold-plated · Four red stones preserved · Length: 3.2 cm · Šaratice near Slavkov, (Brno District) · Moravian Museum, Brno

161. Slender jug with massive handle · Well-baked loess · 5th cent. · Height: 28.0 cm · Ivanovice, near Brno · Moravian Museum, Brno

→

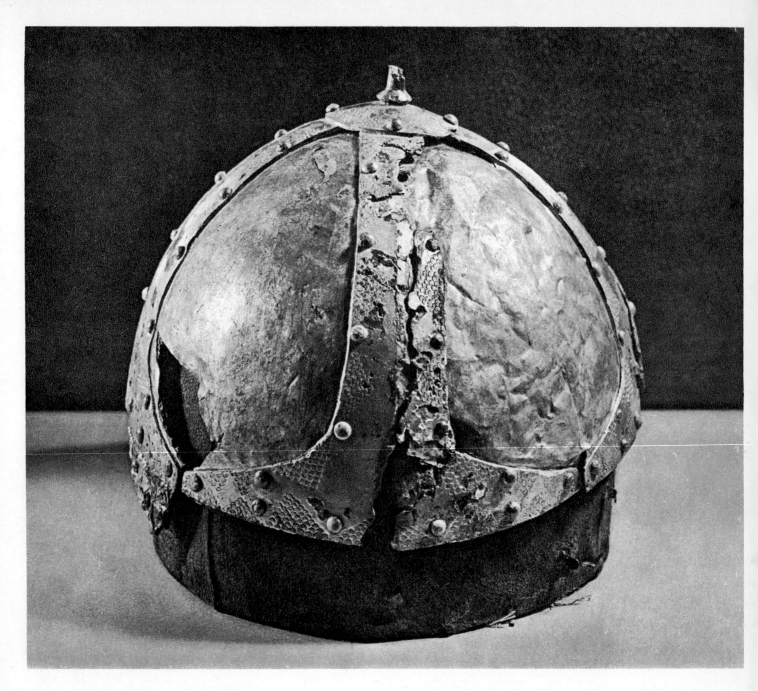

162. Iron helmet with gold- and silver-plated parts, of copper (bronze?) · 6th—7th cent. · Dolní Semerovce, Slovakia · Slovak Museum, Bratislava

XX. Oriental textile preserved in the sacristy of St. Vitus's Cathedral in Prague · According to Prof. Cibulka, it is of Syrian or Byzantine origin, shows the direct influence of Persian designs, and dates from about 600 A. D. It has been preserved by chance, having been used to line the covers of The Gospels from the 9th century · Numerous remains of real silk in Slavonic graves in Staré Město-Uherské Hradiště testify to the importation into the country of Oriental textiles in the 9th century   ·/. →

163. Iron helmet with gold- and silver-plated parts, of copper (bronze?) · 6th—7th cent. · Dolní Semerovce, Slovakia · Slovak Museum, Bratislava

THE OLDEST SLAVS

164. Vase of the Prague Type · Pottery ·
Slav Culture. 4th—5th cent. · Height: 21.0 cm
· Velatice, near Brno · Moravian Museum,
Brno

165. + 166. Two-handled vessel and jug of
fine loess and well-baked clay · 7th cent. ·
Avar-Slav Culture · Height: 18.5 cm; 21.5 cm
· Děvínská Nová Ves · Slovak Museum,
Bratislava   ·/. →

170. Shallow vessel of baked loess · Slav Culture · 8th cent. · Height: 12.0 cm · Dolní Dunajovice (Mikulov District) · Moravian Museum, Brno

169. Barrel-shaped vessel with everted rims and incised design · Pottery · Slav Culture · 7th cent. · Height: 16.7 cm. · Děvínská Nová Ves · Slovak Museum, Bratislava ←

167. + 168. Simple pottery built up by hand with incised ornament · Avar-Slav Culture · 7th cent. · Height: 12.0 cm; 11.0 cm · Holiare (Čalovo District) · Sl. Acad. of Sciences — Arch. Inst., Nitra ·/. ←

171. Gilded bronze metal-work, with orna-
ment showing zoomorphic stylisation · Slav
Culture · 7th cent. · Dimensions: diameters:
6.2 cm; 3.4 cm; sides: 2.2 × 3.2 × 3.3 cm ·
Radvaň nad Dunajem. Slovakia · Slovak
Museum, Bratislava

XXI. Oriental textile preserved in the sacristy
of. St. Vitus's Cathedral in Prague · See also
colour pl. XX and XXII.   ·/. →

172. Gilded bronze metal-work, with ornament showing zoomorphic stylisation · Slav
Culture. 7th cent. · Dimensions: diameter
6.2 cm · Radvaň nad Dunajem. Slovakia ·
Slovak Museum, Bratislava

SLAVS FROM THE IXth TO THE XIIth CENTURY

173. Slim vessel decorated with three parallel
bands of engraved wavy lines · Baked loess ·
Slav Culture · 9th cent. · Height: 19.0 cm ·
Dolní Věstonice (Mikulov District) · Moravian Museum, Brno

174. Vessel with expressively profiled neck
and incised wavy line · Slav Culture · 9th
cent. · Height: 15.3 cm · Dolní Věstonice
(Mikulov District) · Moravian Museum, Brno

175. Two-handled bottle · Baked loess of
very fine texture · Slav Culture · 2nd half of
9th cent. · Height: 20.8 cm · Staré Město-
Uherské Hradiště · Moravian Museum, Brno

→

176. Iron-work on an oval bucket and flat flask of fine loess · Slav Culture · 2nd half of 9th cent. · Heights: 25.3 cm; 20.0 cm · Staré Město-Uherské Hradiště · Moravian Museum, Brno

177. Iron-work on wooden bucket · Slav Culture, 2nd half of 9th cent. · Height: 10.5 cm · Rebešovice (Židlochovice District) · Cz. Acad. of Sciences — Arch. Inst., Brno

179. Silver finger-ring and gold earring, richly beaded · Slav Culture, 2nd half of 9th cent. · Diameter of ring: 1.8 cm · Height of earrings: 2.5 cm · Staré Město-Uherské Hradiště · Moravian Museum, Brno

178. Bone whistle with encurved ornament · Slav Culture, 2nd half of 9th cent. · Length: 9.5 cm · Staré Město-Uherské Hradiště · Moravian Museum, Brno

180. Slav jewellery · Finger-ring and ornamental button · Silver · Gilded bronze · 10th
cent. · Height: 2.5 cm; 3.9 cm · Lichoceves,
Budeč, Bohemia · National Museum, Prague

XXII. The cover of The Gospels from the
9th cent. · It is of gilded copper ornamented
with semi-precious stones · The carving is
usually dated as belonging to the 4th cent.
A. D. · The sacristy of St. Vitus's, Prague ·
Dimensions: (cover) 27.5 × 35 cm, (carving)
11.2 × 25.3 cm (see colour pl. XX and XXI)

181. Back of a gold pendant set with an antique cameo · Slav Culture. 10th cent. · Axis of pendant 3.3 × 2.7 cm (see colour pl. XVIII.) · Želénky by Duchcov · National Museum, Prague

182. Finely engraved clasp. · Bone · Old Hungarian. 10th cent. · Length: 10 cm · Sereď-Máčanské vršky · Sl. Acad. of Sciences — Arch. Inst., Nitra   →

184. Buckle-plate and buckle-bow, richly decorated with silver embossed metal work · Slav chieftain's grave. 10th cent. · Dimensions: height: 6.2 cm; 9.3 cm, axis of the buckle: 5.9 ×3.9 cm · Kolín · National Museum, Prague

183. Gold-plated silver chalice · Slav chieftain's grave. 10th cent. · Height of original part preserved: 9.0 cm · Kolín · National Museum, Prague ←

185. Badly damaged bone-urn (ossuary),
with embossed deer and bird · Silver · Slav
Culture. 10th cent. · Length of preserved
part: 6.6 cm · Želénky by Duchcov · National Museum, Prague

186. Zoomorphic vessel · Pottery ·Slav Culture. 11th—12th cent. · Height: 12.8 cm ·
Čáslav · Museum in Čáslav

188. Bronze sculpture: The Crucified Man ·
Slav Culture. 12th cent. · Height: 7.8 cm ·
Znojmo · Moravian Museum, Brno

187. Silver Agnus Dei · Slav Culture. 10th
cent. · Height: 2.8 cm · Komárov by Opava
· National Museum, Prague   ←

189. Bone comb decorated with figures ·
Slav Culture. 12th cent. · Length: 11.3 cm ·
Uherský Brod · Museum in Uherský Brod

PREHISTORIC ART

Including some recent cave-culture
discoveries and subsequent developments
up to Roman times

This book deals with prehistoric culture in certain areas from the Middle Palaeolithic period to Roman times.

Some of the most dramatic discoveries described, such as the Old Stone Age cave habitation at Předmostí, with its glyptic art and unique multiple burial, and the great Bronze Age funerary holocaust of the 6th Century B. C. at Adamov, were made just before the recent war and are as yet little known even to specialists in this country.

Much of the other material will also be quite new to the majority of people interested in the subject, and it may confidently be said that the splendid reproductions are themselves unique and of fascinating interest both to the lay reader and the expert.